A DANGEROUS OCCUPATION

" A Dangerous Occupation "
has been published as a Limited Edition of 750 copies,
of which this book is Number *289*

FRONT COVER:- HMS *BARRY* in the Gulf of Salonika. (Detail from an original oil painting by Chris Collard).

BACK COVER:- HMS *DEVONIA* explodes a mine in her sweep.

Able-Seaman W. H. Sully. HMS *GLEN USK.*

Bill Sully was born in Watchet, Somerset, in January 1893. As a boy he ran away to sea on a small merchant ship. On the outbreak of the First World War he joined the Royal Navy and served aboard HMS *GLEN USK*. During one of her early minesweeping sorties, just before a mine was exploded in her sweep, he failed to hear the order to put in ear-plugs. As a result one of his ear-drums became perforated. On a subsequent occasion, again he failed to hear a similar order which resulted in him becoming almost totally deaf. He was discharged because of deafness and returned to his home town of Watchet, where he found work in the paper mill. He married his wife, Lilian, shortly afterwards. His love of the sea remained with him and he was a keen inshore fisherman; in his later years he could often be seen in his small boat, fishing along the coast between Blue Anchor and St. Audries. He died on 13 August 1958 and is buried at St. Decumens Church, Watchet.

Photograph and information kindly supplied by Keith Thomas.

A DANGEROUS OCCUPATION

WHITE FUNNELS – VOLUME THREE

A story of Paddle Minesweepers in the First World War

BY

CHRIS COLLARD

The drifters they caught submarines and the paddlers were willing
To drop their trade of making trippers seasick for a shilling,
To join the trawlers sweeping mines, and, aided by the yachts,
Their harvest was a good one as the channel yielded lots.

From one of the "Ballads of the Dover Patrol".

WHEELHOUSE BOOKS.
4, Ty Mawr Close,
Rumney,
Cardiff.
CF3 3BU.

PUBLISHED BY WHEELHOUSE BOOKS
PRODUCED BY WILPRINT GROUP LTD.
BOOKBINDING BY PRINCIPAL BOOKBINDERS LTD
COVER DESIGN BY PETER H. JONES, WILPRINT GROUP LTD.

ISBN 0-9534275-1-X

CONTENTS

ACKNOWLEDGEMENTS

I wish to express my sincere thanks to the following institutions and individuals for their assistance in the preparation of this volume:-

The Public Records Office, Kew, Surrey - the repository of the Admiralty records.
The Bristol Records Office - the repository of the records of P. & A. Campbell Ltd.
The Imperial War Museum.
The National Maritime Museum.
The Naval Historical Branch of the Ministry of Defence.
The Admiralty Library.
The Guildhall Library.
The Royal Commission on Historic Manuscripts.
The Glasgow University Archives.
The Welsh Industrial and Maritime Museum.
The Cardiff Public Libraries.

Dr. Donald Anderson; Mr. Laurence Dunn; Mr. Victor Gray; Mr. Alfred Harvey; Mr. John Niblett; Mr. Sydney Robinson; Mr. Peter Southcombe; Mr. Keith Thomas.

The late Messrs. H. A. Allen, Howard Davies, Ernest Dumbleton, Edwin Keen, Graham Langmuir and Capt. L. G. A. Thomas.

My particular thanks, once again, must go to Mr. George Owen, not only for his knowledge and expertise which have readily been at my disposal, but also for much practical help, particularly in the meticulous checking of my manuscript.

SOURCES

The major sources of information on which this book is based are the Admiralty records deposited in the Public Records Office. The relevant classes are ADM1 and ADM116 - the main series of papers concerning the administration of naval affairs; ADM137 - operational reports from ships, squadrons and stations from 1914 to 1919; ADM53 - ships log books; ADM176 - photographs of ships; ADM182 - Admiralty Fleet Orders; ADM177 - Navy Lists; ADM167 - Board of Admiralty Minutes and Memoranda.

The photographs reproduced in this volume are taken from my collection. Those of identified origin are credited accordingly, but in most cases it has been impossible to establish the exact identity of the photographers. I hope that this "omnibus" acknowledgement will serve as an appreciation of all those people in recognition of their work and their valuable contributions to this history.

Other books by Chris Collard

White Funnels - The Story of Campbells Steamers 1946-1968.
Special Excursions - The Story of Campbells Steamers 1919-1939.
P. & A. Campbell Pleasure Steamers 1887-1945.
P. & A. Campbell Pleasure Steamers from 1946.
Bristol Channel Shipping-The Twilight Years.

Forthcoming Publications

White Funnels - The Story of Campbells Steamers 1946-1968. (2nd Edition)
On Admiralty Service - The Story of Campbells Steamers in World War Two.

For further details write to:-
Chris Collard, Wheelhouse Books, 4 Ty Mawr Close, Rumney, Cardiff. CF3 3BU.

INTRODUCTION

Two paddle steamers, "A" and "B", were engaged in minesweeping operations a short distance apart. The commander of A, standing on the wing of the bridge, heard a voice which shouted, "Oi!". The commander, looking around, was unable to ascertain the whereabouts of the voice. "Oi!", it shouted again, but the commander was once again unable to trace its source. With its third "Oi!" the voice added, "Tell the bloke up topsides to stop the bloody engines, I can't get out of 'ere!"

The commander found that the voice belonged to a frightened face peering out of B's paddle box. With exemplary Royal Naval aplomb, A signalled to B, "There is a man hailing me from your paddle-box. What is the matter with him?"

It was discovered that the man was a newly-recruited Merchant Navy fireman who had gone into the paddle-box, for reasons best known to himself, while the two ships had stopped to shorten their sweep wires in order to turn. As soon as the engines were re-started and the paddle revolved, his retreat was cut off and he flattened himself against the facing of the paddle-box, where he was pinned like a spider trying to get through an electric fan. When the ships were stopped, he extricated himself without difficulty, little the worse for his experience apart from being soaked to the skin!

This true story illustrates that there can be moments of "comedy" even under the most adverse circumstances. And if ever a preponderance of adversity predominated, it was during the Great War at sea. It was not a war of dramatic naval encounters - hopes of a latter day Trafalgar were unfulfilled - it was a war against those insidious enemies, the mine and the torpedo, both of which brought their own terrors no less horrifying than those of the hideous war of attrition fought in the trenches.

During the course of the hostilities Germany laid in excess of 43,000 mines in all parts of the world, principally in the North Sea and around the British Isles; there was hardly an important harbour, channel or estuary which was not mined at least once in the hope of destroying allied shipping. The lion's share of minesweeping operations, therefore, fell upon Great Britain.

In common with many other excursion vessels, the paddle steamers of P. & A. Campbell's White Funnel Fleet were hired by the Admiralty to act, principally, as minesweepers. Unlike the major part of the Mercantile Marine, the ships were commissioned into the Royal Navy, flew the White Ensign and were manned, mainly, by Royal Naval Reservists.

Their tasteful peacetime colours became drab warship grey; guns and minesweeping apparatus filled their decks where, only months before, crowds of holidaymakers had enjoyed the sunshine and sea air. The arduous duties which they were now called upon to perform could hardly have been in greater contrast to those for which they were intended, and some did not return. Yet, their work was vital and was of inestimable value to the war effort.

Contrary to its peacetime role, the fleet no longer acted in isolation but played its part in a wider field of operations. This work, therefore, views the activities of its steamers in the context of a broader sphere.

A wealth of hitherto unpublished material has been revealed by extensive research, but despite exhaustive efforts there is no doubt that many questions still remain unanswered. Nevertheless, it is hoped that the pages which follow will shed some light on the darkness which has surrounded the steamers' wartime adventures and bestow the full honour and gratitude, so richly deserved, upon the men who gallantly manned them, fought, and gave their lives for their country and its future generations.

The timetable of the final sailings of the White Funnel Fleet from Bristol in 1914

PROLOGUE

The White Funnel Fleet of 1914

PS *GLEN ROSA*, (1877), leaving Brighton in 1912.

PS *WAVERLEY*, (1885), arriving at Eastbourne in 1911. (W. A. Pelly).

PS *RAVENSWOOD*, (1891), arriving at Eastbourne in 1912. (W. A. Pelly).

PS *ALBION*, (1893), arriving at Eastbourne, 1913/1914. (W. A. Pelly).

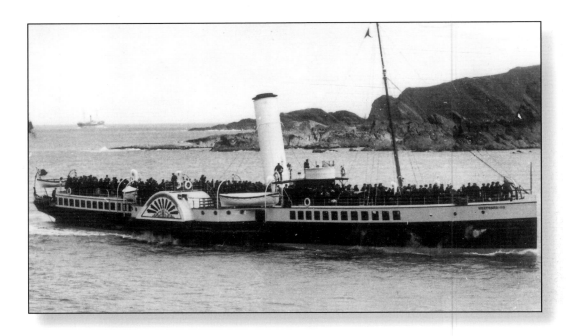

PS *WESTWARD HO*, (1894), arriving at Ilfracombe, 1913/1914.

PS *CAMBRIA*, (1895), off Newquay (Cornwall) on 23rd July 1913.

PS *BRITANNIA*, (1896), arriving at Weston-Super-Mare, 1913/1914.

PS *BRIGHTON QUEEN*, (1897), in the Solent, 1913/1914.

PS *DEVONIA*, (1905), in the River Avon, 1913/1914.

PS *BARRY*, (1907), arriving at Ilfracombe, 1913/1914.

PS *LADY ISMAY*, (1911), in the River Avon on 24th June 1914. (E. Stephens).

PS *GLEN AVON*, (1912), in the Cumberland Basin, Bristol, in 1914. (E. Stephens).

PS *GLEN USK*, (1914), at Newport in 1914. (W. Clifton).

STRATAGEMS AND SPOILS

"...the rascals will never come out but will
only send out minelayers and submarines...."
Rear-Admiral David Beatty. October 1914.

At 06.30 on Monday 20th July 1914 the Royal Yacht, *VICTORIA AND ALBERT*, with His Majesty King George V aboard, sailed from Portsmouth harbour and anchored in Spithead, amid the might of the British Royal Navy: the ships of the Grand Fleet had assembled for the Royal Naval Review. At 08.30 the Lords Commissioners of the Admiralty and the Commander-in-Chief, Portsmouth, boarded the Royal Yacht which then proceeded to an anchorage in the vicinity of the Nab Tower, to the east of the Isle of Wight. There the Royal Party watched Rear-Admiral David Beatty's 1st Battlecruiser Squadron lead the fleet to sea. King George V is reputed to have said, after the ships· had passed, "I am proud of my Navy".

The splendour of the occasion was, however, over-shadowed by the deteriorating political situation in Europe, and the prospect of imminent conflict; a prospect which had persuaded the Admiralty to hold a trial mobilisation of the fleet prior to its assembly for the review, instead of the usual summer manoeuvres. The fleet had also been ordered not to disperse after the review but to hold itself in readiness for the crisis which appeared inevitable. After its departure from Spithead on 20th July the major part of the Grand Fleet anchored in Portland harbour. Two weeks later the ships were at war!

The complex events which led to the outbreak of the Great War culminated in Germany's invasion of Belgium on Bank Holiday Monday 3rd August 1914. Great Britain sent Germany an ultimatum demanding the withdrawal of her troops, which was ignored, and at 22.30 on Tuesday 4th August King George V held a privy council at Buckingham Palace which sanctioned the proclamation of a state of war between the two countries. The Admiralty immediately signalled to all Royal Naval ships, "Commence hostilities against Germany".

On Tuesday 28th July the ships of the Grand Fleet had been ordered to war stations. The First Lord of the Admiralty, Winston Churchill, ordered full mobilisation on the night of 1st/2nd August which was approved by the cabinet on the following day, by which time the Grand Fleet had reached its base at Scapa Flow in the Orkneys.

The King had also signed a proclamation calling up the men of the Royal Naval Reserve, the Royal Fleet Reserve and the Royal Naval Volunteer Reserve. Notices were published in most London and provincial newspapers which included the following:-

"Notice is hereby given by their Lordships that all Naval and Marine Pensioners under the age of 55, all men of the RNR, RFR and RNVR are to proceed forthwith to the ship or establishment already notified them... Men who, through absence at sea or for other unavoidable cause, are unable to join immediately are to report themselves as soon as possible. Any man who fails to report himself without delay in compliance with this order will be liable to arrest as a deserter, and any pensioner will also be liable to forfeit his pension."

92*/an

AT THE COURT AT BUCKINGHAM PALACE,

The 3rd day of August, 1914.

PRESENT,

THE KING'S MOST EXCELLENT MAJESTY IN COUNCIL.

WHEREAS there was this day read at the Board a Memorial from the Right Honourable the Lords Commissioners of the Admiralty, in the words following, viz.:—

> "WHEREAS we are of opinion that the present state of Public Affairs justifies Officers of the Reserved and Retired Lists being called into Active Service temporarily; we would humbly submit that Your Majesty will be pleased to authorize us to call on such Officers to hold themselves in readiness for Active Service, and to sanction our employing any of such Officers as we may think fit. We would also submit that compulsory retirement from the Active List on account of age be suspended in such cases as we think fit."

HIS MAJESTY, having taken the said Memorial into consideration, was pleased, by and with the advice of His Privy Council, to approve of what is therein proposed. And the Right Honourable the Lords Commissioners of the Admiralty are to give the necessary directions herein accordingly.

ALMERIC FITZROY.

Printed by EYRE and SPOTTISWOODE, Ltd.,
Printers to the King's most Excellent Majesty. 1914.
For His Majesty's Stationery Office.

(33)23375 200 & 1 8/14 E & S (8)

The Proclamation of King George V sanctioning the mobilisation of the officers of the Royal Naval Reserve and Retired Lists.

PRO Ref: ADM1/8388/228

On 8th August 1914 Mr Churchill wrote to the Admiralty departments:-

"For the present, departments should proceed on the general assumption that the war will last one year, of which the greatest effort should be concentrated on the first six months, and all arrangements for the construction of vessels, works and supplies should be made with this period in view. Later on it may be necessary to extend the war period, in which case the arrangements made now could be modified to include work which is too far from completion now to stand in the way of more urgent services, and to provide for the permanent supply and maintenance of the fleet.

Although the transition from peace to war conditions must be attended with a certain amount of emergency action, that period is passing, and the adoption of regular and careful methods is enjoined on all departments. In particular, thrift and scrupulous attention to details are the marks of efficient administration in war. After all these years the Admiralty is now on its trial as an organisation and the First Lord is very anxious that rigorous action should be combined with strict economy, so that the work of the department may subsequently become a model.

The work done by all in the last ten days is admirable."

Opening Moves.

The German Battlefleet - the High Seas Fleet - had assembled off Wilhelmshaven, in the mouth of the River Jade. The orders issued to its Commander-in-Chief, Admiral Friedrich von Ingenohl, were that no attempt should be made to engage the superior forces of the Grand Fleet at that stage, in the firm belief that the army would defeat the British Expeditionary Force on land and that the war would be "all over by Christmas". The extent of German naval strategy was confined initially to defensive patrolling off Heligoland in expectation of Great Britain establishing a close blockade of her seaports.

As early as 1912 the Admiralty had decided against such an action, realising that it would afford Germany an ideal opportunity for attacking units of the Royal Navy with mines and torpedoes, thus leading, in time, to a reduction in the size of the Grand Fleet and a more even balance of forces. Instead a distant blockade was imposed by way of two defensive barriers; one across the Dover Straits, patrolled by light forces, and another extending from Scotland to Norway, backed up by the Grand Fleet. These boundaries sealed Germany's entrances and exits to and from the Atlantic Ocean and led to a serious curtailment of the export and import of food and raw materials on which Germany relied.

Early on the morning of Wednesday 5th August, only a matter of hours after the declaration of war, the German steamer, *KONIGIN LUISE*, sailed across the North Sea from her base at Emden. She was a former excursion steamer which ran between Hamburg and Heligoland in peacetime and which had been rapidly converted into an unarmed minelayer. She was seen by the skipper of the Lowestoft fishing smack, *LITTLE BOYS*, "dropping things over her stern" some thirty miles east of the Suffolk coastal town of Southwold. The 'things" were 180 mines. During her run for home she encountered a flotilla of British destroyers, led by the light-cruiser, *AMPHION*, and owing to her lack of armament her crew had little alternative other than to scuttle her. At 06.35 next morning, on her return to Harwich, the *AMPHION* herself struck one of the *KONIGIN LUISE'S* mines and sank with a loss of 151 lives; the first British Naval casualty of the war.

Placed as it was, in international waters, the minefield was just as likely to destroy neutral ships as British but there is evidence that the *KONIGIN LUISE* laid her cargo further seaward than the German Admiralty intended, and that her actual orders were to mine the approaches to Harwich, a legitimate operation provided the mines were laid within three miles of the coast; the principal being to block the harbour and prevent the exit of the enemy's ships.

Nevertheless, Germany continued the practice of laying mines in the open sea, in defiance of the Hague Convention, which opposed the indiscriminate laying of mines outside an enemy's territorial waters. When Britain formally protested Germany excused herself on the plea that the International agreement for the restriction of minelaying to territorial waters was binding only if all belligerents had ratified it. Russia was a belligerent and had not ratified the Hague Convention; therefore, said Germany, she could lay mines wherever she liked. This policy was adopted irrespective of the principles of humanity which had been so earnestly proclaimed by the chief German delegate at the Hague Conference of 1907.

The Royal Navy's minesweeping force, at the outbreak of the war, consisted of nothing more than six old, converted torpedo-gunboats. This unreadiness for minesweeping on a large scale emanated from its misplaced trust in Germany conforming to the principles of the Hague Convention. It was therefore imperative that other vessels should be pressed into service to meet the minelaying threat in order to clear the coastal traffic lanes for the free movement of sea-borne commerce.

Improvisation.

In 1907 it had been suggested that, if necessary, trawlers could be used for minesweeping purposes and by 1912 the trawler section of the Royal Naval Reserve had been established. It allowed for the vessels to be taken up as required, equipped, manned and pressed into service with great rapidity. Trawlers had the advantage of possessing the apparatus necessary for the handling of nets which would serve equally well for sweep wires, and by Saturday 8th August 1914, 94 trawlers had been mobilised and were sweeping for mines. Within two weeks nearly another hundred had been requisitioned.

They were manned by their usual crews of fishermen; tough, hardy men inured to every hardship of the sea and accustomed to pleasing themselves. Would they be amenable to naval discipline or would they prove to be an element of discord? The question was answered by Capt. W. M. Bruce, a Royal Naval Reserve officer who worked with minesweepers throughout the war:-

> " In short, they were admirable! They rapidly attained the initiative and the resource that enabled their arduous and dangerous work to be carried out without intermission. I have worked with all classes and many nationalities of men in all corners of the world, but I never want, or hope, to work with a finer lot than the crews of the minesweeping trawlers."

DANGER WARNING

MINES

SHOULD NEVER BE TOUCHED

but should be **IMMEDIATELY** reported to the

nearest **COAST GUARD** or **POLICE**

REWARDS

are paid for the first

GENUINE REPORT OF A MINE

which leads to it being secured or destroyed.

NOTE:

Mines are usually round or pear-shaped.
They usually have **FOUR** or more **HORNS**
or Spikes at one end, and at the other end
a screwed-in plug. Also a screwed-in plate
at one side.

The mine warning which was posted in profusion in coastal towns and villages.

PRO Ref: ADM137/2265

However, the acceptance of naval discipline was not without its difficulties, sometimes of an amusing nature. On one occasion a minesweeping trawler had become parted from her consorts and sent off a wireless message saying - "Enemy aircraft 300 feet overhead, dropping bombs". The message was received by a requisitioned yacht whose commander proceeded at once into the minefield to assist. There was considerable difficulty in locating the trawler, as all signals by wireless remained unanswered. Finally she was found, with her lifeboats away, and the following conversation with their occupants took place by semaphore:-

Commander: What are you doing?
Reply: Picking up fish killed by bomb explosions.
Commander: Why don't you answer my wireless signals?
Reply: Wireless operator is collecting fish in one of the boats!

Before the end of August 1914 German surface minelayers had laid three large minefields off the east coast of England - off Southwold, off the Humber and off the Tyne. No more than 12 mines out of the several hundreds laid, and not yet properly located, had been swept up and destroyed. For this meagre result 6 trawlers had been blown up with the loss of half of their crews.

It was evident that trawlers, though excellent minesweepers in many respects, drew too much water with their draught of up to 14ft. and with their speed of about 8 knots, were too slow. Consideration was urgently given to other types of ships which might be suitable and available for the purpose.

Pioneers.

In early August 1914, laid up in the Floating Harbour at Bristol, at the end of their curtailed season, were most of the steamers of the White Funnel Fleet. They came under the careful scrutiny of a naval lieutenant, Arthur L. Sanders; as a Bristol man he was familiar with the steamers and was well aware of their speed, manoeuvrability and shallow draught. It is uncertain whether or not Lieut. Sanders was solely responsible for suggesting to the Admiralty that they would make ideal minesweepers, but there is no doubt that he was the prime mover behind their initial trials.

Of the steamers available it appeared that the *BRIGHTON QUEEN* and the *DEVONIA* would be the most suitable. Accordingly they were taken in hand by the shipyard workers and prepared for minesweeping trials. Their conversion entailed the removal of all non-essential apparatus and fittings from above and below decks. A powerful winch replaced the stern capstan of each ship. The sweep wire was coiled around the central drum of the winch and then passed through a pulley fixed to the underside of the top bar of an "A"-shaped steel frame, between 15 and 20 feet high. This was known as the gallows, and was placed towards the after end of the quarter deck, inclined at an angle of about 20° outwards over the steamer's stern.

By mid-August 1914 their civilian colours had been replaced by warship grey and the two ships were undergoing minesweeping trials in the Bristol Channel. They proved eminently suitable for the task and their commissioning into the Royal Navy towards the end of the month pioneered the requisitioning of many more of the country's pleasure steamers.

The act of commissioning a ship into the Royal Navy is rich with history. The ceremony, however, varies according to the status of the ship in the Fleet. In the case of the wartime hired paddle steamers, while the Admiralty did not deny the vital importance of their duties, the ceremony was minimal. Essentially a ship was in commission when an officer appointed to that ship arrived on board and gave the order to hoist the white commissioning pendant and the white ensign. The ship's books would then be opened for the entry of the details of her officers and crew.

This procedure, as short and simple as it was, changed the character and purpose of the excursion steamers so completely. No greater contrast could be imagined than the transition they experienced between peace and war.

A letter from the Admiralty to the Under Secretary of State at the Foreign Office, dated November 1871, detailing the process of putting a ship officially into commission, ends with the following paragraph:-

> "The official sign of a commissioned ship of war is the carrying of the appointed colours; and that a ship is commissioned as a British ship of war when any officer holding a commission in HM Navy, having been appointed directly or indirectly by the Government to serve on board ship, shall have gone on board and hoisted the colours prescribed for HM Ships and vessels of War."

At the time of their commissioning the ships were allocated "Pendant Numbers" for identification purposes. Those of HMS *BRIGHTON QUEEN* and HMS *DEVONIA* were 181 and 182 respectively.

The two ships left Bristol on Wednesday 30th September 1914, with Lieut. Sanders in command of the *BRIGHTON QUEEN*, for Devonport, where they were fully fitted out and armed for their forthcoming duties. While at the naval dockyard a number of their engine parts were stripped down for inspection by the Admiralty surveyor. It is worthy of note that on inspecting the paddle shaft bearings of the *DEVONIA* he stated that they "looked like new" - an example of how well the ships were constructed and maintained in those days! They were then sent to their first war time base - the east coast port of Grimsby, from where they began sweeping operations in the North Sea in mid-December.

Mines and Minesweeping.

A mine was a spherical buoy roughly three feet in diameter and contained about 300lbs. of guncotton, TNT, or amatol. This explosive, together with the firing batteries, occupied about half of the space of the buoy, the rest being used as an air chamber to give it buoyancy. On top of the mine, on the outside, were a number of lead "horns", each about six inches long and just over an inch in diameter. Inside each horn was a glass tube containing a chemical mixture. A blow of about 50lbs. or more would fracture a horn, the glass tube would smash and release its liquid which would energise the battery. The battery then fired a detonator which, in turn, detonated the explosive, which destroyed or seriously damaged the object which struck the mine and crumpled the horn in the first instance.

Seen from the Mardyke Wharf, Bristol, in mid-August 1914, the *DEVONIA* is being warped across the Floating Harbour after being painted in warship grey at Charles Hill's yard.

Now commissioned into the Royal Navy and flying the White Ensign, HMS *DEVONIA* awaits her departure for minesweeping trials on Tuesday 25th August 1914. Several members of her crew appear to be familiarising themselves with the kite, while others concentrate on the newly-fitted winch. At the after end of the promenade deck, just behind the gallows, the officer seen in naval uniform is probably Lieut. Arthur Sanders, and the man next to him, looking away from the camera, appears to be Capt. Peter Cambell.

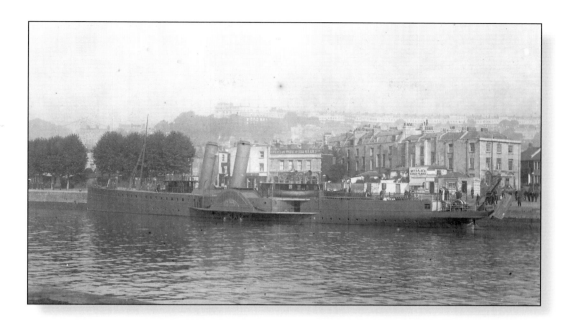

HMS *DEVONIA* in the Cumberland Basin, Tuesday 25th August 1914.

HMS *DEVONIA* steaming down the Avon Gorge on Tuesday 25th August 1914; a familiar scene made so poignantly different by the absence of her peacetime colours and the advent of warship grey. Her repainting, however, is not quite complete - the after end of the saloon bulkhead and the ventilator above it have been missed by the shipyard painters.

HMS *BRIGHTON QUEEN* (left), and HMS *DEVONIA* in the Cumberland Basin, on Wednesday 30th September 1914; a sad day indeed for the passengers about to board the two steamers. They were the families of the ships' personnel, who were allowed to make the short journey from the basin to Hotwells Landing Stage where they disembarked after bidding farewell to their loved ones.

HMS *BRIGHTON QUEEN* in the Cumberland Basin, 30th September 1914, with Lieut. Arthur Sanders on the port bridge wing.

HMS *BRIGHTON QUEEN* leaving the Cumberland Basin, 30th September 1914.

Having discharged her passengers at Hotwells Landing Stage, just upstream from the Clifton Suspension Bridge, HMS *BRIGHTON QUEEN* leaves Bristol for Devonport, 30th September 1914.

HMS *DEVONIA* leaving Bristol for Devonport, 30th September 1914.

Mines were laid in fields or groups in pre-arranged positions, each mine being anchored to the sea bed by way of a mooring wire and sinker. The mine case entered the water and the sinker descended towards the sea bed with the mooring wire unreeling from its drum as it travelled downwards. Beneath the sinker was another weight, known as a plummet, attached to the sinker by a chain. The chain was adjusted in length according to the distance below the surface of the water at which the mine was required. The plummet hit the bottom first and the slackening of its chain automatically locked the drum on the main sinker and prevented any more wire from running out. The main sinker then came into play and pulled the mine itself down to the pre-arranged depth below the surface.

Minesweeping, in its simplest form, consisted of towing a sunken sweep wire between two ships, two or more pairs working together to cover as wide a front as possible. The sweep wire was much the same size as the mine mooring, usually about two inches in circumference; however, in order that the mine should be quickly cut free from its moorings and float to the surface for destruction, what was known as "serrated" sweep wire was used. Instead of the wire being laid up in the usual manner, it had one irregular strand which, when under strain, exercised a sawing effect on the mooring wire. Sometimes, however, it was necessary for the vessels themselves to resort to a sawing manoeuvre - one ship would reduce speed to slow and the other increase to full. Then, when the leading ship was a short distance ahead of the rear vessel the latter would increase speed and the leader reduce. After doing this two or three times the mine moorings were sure to be cut by sliding to and fro along the sweep wire.

A frequent problem was the parting of sweep wires. Although spare wire was carried, broken sweeps did not hold up the job; in fact, so expert did the men become that in less than 15 minutes two of them would have repaired the wire having made use of the "cut" splice - not the neatest of joins perhaps, but effective.

Each minesweeper dragged a "kite", a heavy, "L" shaped appliance, about ten feet in length and weighing about one ton which, when towed from the steam winch, sank to the depth permitted by the amount of wire paid out. The sweep wire passed through slings on the kites, towed by a pair of vessels, thus forming a span of wire beneath the surface, roughly parallel to the sea bed.

Capt. C. C. Bell DSO. RN., an experienced minesweeper commander, said of the kite:-

> "It was the blessing, or more often, the curse of sweeping. A good kite, well balanced, with the slings adjusted correctly, would dive straight down and take up its depth and stay there. Perhaps for a week it would be a model of good behaviour. Then it would become possessed of a devil and behave like a bucking bronco, leaping a dozen feet out of the water, over the sweep wire and down to the depths, then out again to turn over on its back and sulk, when nothing would make it dive. Finally it might have to be hove up, and hours spent in getting all the turns out of the wire. When streamed again it would be a model of good behaviour, until the devil entered into it once again. I know of nothing more exasperating than an evilly-disposed kite!"

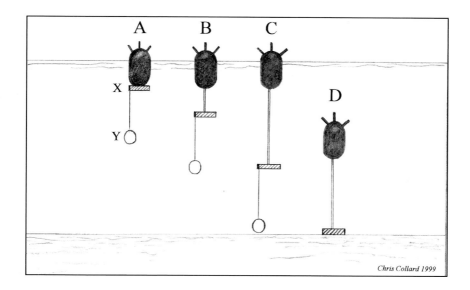

The Method of Minelaying

A. Mine dropped. Plummet runs out to its end.
B. Mine remains on surface. Sinker descending.
C. Mine still on surface. Plummet hits the sea bed and prevents more cable unreeling.
D. Sinker descends and pulls mine with it. The depth of the mine below the surface equals the distance XY on plummet chain in A.

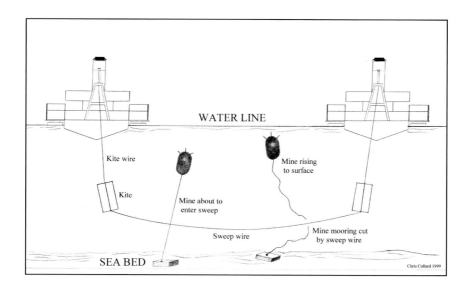

The Method of Minesweeping. (Not to scale).

The sweep wire would be passed from ship to ship by hand, both vessels steaming slowly ahead so close as to be nearly touching. Then, while one of the pair secured the end of the sweep and moved off at an angle to open out the sweeping distance, usually three to five hundred yards, her partner eased out the wire. The kites would then be lowered to the correct depth and the sweepers were ready for work.

The business entailed many hours of hard work and many fruitless days. An officer commented, "It was such a joy to hear a shout from the after deck - 'Mine in the sweep, sir'". It was then necessary to destroy the mine. Orders were for this to be done by gunfire but it was easier said than done. A distance of at least 300 yards had to be maintained, and with the small target bobbing up and down, sometimes submerged, with the ship rolling and pitching, it was a difficult and frustrating task. Frequently the mines were dispatched with rifle fire, either by holing them and causing them to sink, or by hitting one of their horns and causing them to explode. The latter method was to be preferred; it was far more satisfying to see an enormous mushroom of water rising into the air and knowing that the mine would never serve the purpose for which it was laid.

Accuracy of navigation was of prime importance, a minefield wrongly plotted could bring disaster to shipping. Precise station keeping was also paramount while sweeping was in progress. If sweepers were out of position and gaps were left, an area which had been swept, and was therefore supposedly safe, might really have mines left in it and still be dangerous.

A knowledge of tides and their rise and fall was also essential. Mines laid at a certain distance from the sea bottom were closer to the surface at low water and therefore more dangerous to sweepers. Moreover, when the tide was flowing, the current acting on the mine and its mooring rope caused it to be deflected below its set depth and therefore rendered it less dangerous.

In addition to the operational intricacies of minesweeping there was the human factor. Day after day the men faced hours of hard work and drudgery in all weathers. The monotony of the job was accompanied by an overwhelming sense of impending peril and the tension, at times, became unbearable.

The minesweeping service mainly evolved from a collection of fishermen, merchant seamen and volunteers from all walks of life, and gradually expanded into a highly trained, disciplined force revered for its skill and endurance.

Co-ordination.

By the autumn of 1914 every minefield had been discovered by the loss of ships. It was decided that there would have to be a daily, systematic search of all coastal waters and that the actual sweeping should be linked with the control of traffic.

A letter from the Admiralty Secretary to Admiral Sir John Jellicoe, Commander-in-Chief of the Grand Fleet, dated September 13th 1914, states:-

> "I am commanded by my Lords Commissioners of the Admiralty to advise you that they have approved of the following organisation of the Minesweeping service in the area from St. Abbs Head to the South Goodwin, exclusive of the area now worked from the Nore to Harwich....

A Flag Officer will have charge of this service and will be styled 'Admiral Commanding East Coast Minesweepers'. Rear-Admiral E. F. B. Charlton, CB., has been selected for this appointment as from 1st September 1914....

Port Minesweeping Officers will be placed under his orders at Lowestoft, Yarmouth, Grimsby and North Shields...

The Admiral Commanding East Coast Minesweepers will have an office in the Admiralty and will be at liberty to hoist his flag in any vessel under his orders if he goes afloat."

The difficulties and complexities confronting Rear-Admiral Edward Charlton were enormous but he was well known throughout the service as a good, practical organiser with initiative and resource.

The Minesweeping Division of the Naval Staff at the Admiralty became responsible for the drafting and circulation of the "Q" messages - information and instructions regarding the avoidance of mined areas in the North Sea, round about the British Isles and off the north and west coasts of France.

The moment a mine was discovered its position was buoyed, shipping in the vicinity was diverted, and as soon as tidal conditions permitted, the danger area was swept. The text of a "Q" message was sent to the Admiralty by the senior officer on the spot, checked by the Minesweeping Division, then broadcast to all shore stations by land telegram, and to all ships at sea via the Wireless Telegraphy station at Cleethorpes. The average time from the discovery of a mine to the issue of information was little more than an hour.

The system initiated by Rear-Admiral Charlton worked extremely well. Over 4000 such messages were issued throughout the war, and after the scheme became generally known, hardly a vessel that obeyed instructions was sunk by a mine. What losses did occur were due either to a disregard of the instructions, to encountering a freshly laid minefield or to adverse weather conditions.

As the autumn of 1914 gave way to winter, with its cold, gales and heavy seas, the minesweeping force grew and the organisation gradually became perfected under the energetic direction of Rear-Admiral Charlton. He considered it unwise to attempt to clear the outlying minefields during the approaching bad weather. Instead, he took the course of concentrating all his available sweepers further inshore on the approaches to important harbours, and on the regular sweeping of a coastal channel marked by buoys at regular intervals. This fairway, known as "The War Channel", had originated in the cleared area inside the Southwold minefield, laid by the *KONIGIN LUISE* at the outbreak of the war. It was extended at first from the Thames to the Humber and eventually stretched from Portland to the Firth of Forth, a distance of about 540 miles. Every yard of this was swept daily, except in the very worst weather, by the minesweeping forces based at Portland; Portsmouth; the Nore, (Thames Estuary); Dover; Harwich; Lowestoft; the Humber; the Tyne and Granton.

The Grimsby Paddlers.

To assist in the massive operation of sweeping the War Channel further paddle steamers were gradually requisitioned. Of the White Funnel Fleet, the *GLEN AVON*,

LADY ISMAY, WESTWARD HO and *CAMBRIA* were called up; the last named being renamed *CAMBRIDGE,* to avoid confusion with the London and North Western Railway's twin screw vessel of the same name. They were converted, armed and commissioned at Bristol, and left their home port on Wednesday 2nd December bound for Devonport but had to put into Ilfracombe for shelter from the severe weather conditions. However, the heavy swell running into the harbour caused them to range violently at the pier and, to avoid damage, they were forced to put back to Barry. After a further call at Ilfracombe on Monday 7th December they proceeded to Devonport and eventually made their way to the east coast, encountering much bad weather on the way, to join the *BRIGHTON QUEEN* and *DEVONIA* at Grimsby. The six steamers were known as the "Grimsby Paddlers" and were placed under the command of the Port Minesweeping Officer, Captain Frances E. Massey-Dawson. Although administered as a single unit the flotilla was frequently split up and, as circumstances demanded, the ships were deployed at a variety of east coast ports between Grimsby and the Thames Estuary.

Raiders.

On the afternoon of Monday 2nd November, under the command of Vice-Admiral Franz von Hipper, the battle-cruisers *SEYDLITZ, MOLTKE, VON DER TANN* and *BLUCHER,* supported by four cruisers, left the River Jade and made a dash across the North Sea to carry out a surprise bombardment of Yarmouth at dawn on the following day. Within an hour of opening fire the ships turned for home. The purpose of this seemingly futile operation was made clear when a British submarine struck a mine while trying to attack the retreating enemy. The bombardment was a cover for the laying of 130 mines in scattered groups in the vicinity of Smith's Knoll, about 25 miles east of Cromer, on the coast of Norfolk; a minefield which took a serious toll of fishing craft.

A similar raid took place just over a month later when, shortly after dawn on Wednesday 16th December, German battle-cruisers bombarded East and West Hartlepool, Whitby and Scarborough, killing 120 people, wounding 400 and inflicting severe damage on these coastal towns. Once again, under cover of the bombardment, over 100 mines were laid, this time by the light cruiser, *KOLBERG,* in Filey Bay, near Scarborough. The minefield had been laid right in the path of coastal shipping and the sea off Scarborough was said to have been strewn with mines; in fact, never afterwards, throughout the whole course of the war, were mines discovered in such profusion, so close together!

Capt. Massey-Dawson immediately issued orders for the clearing of the minefield and dispatched a fleet of trawlers and drifters, northward from Bridlington. The flotilla was under the command of a retired naval officer, Lieut. Godfrey Parsons, whose flagship was trawler No. 58, the *PASSING.* Shortly after dawn on 19th December 1914, as the ships crossed Filey Bay with their sweeps out, the stillness of the calm morning was shattered by a heavy explosion. Further detonations followed and within five minutes numerous mines had been swept up or had exploded in the trawlers sweeps. The scene was one of complete mayhem! Two trawlers had been mined - No 99, the *ORIANDA,* had sunk, and the *PASSING* was badly holed, on fire and blowing off dense clouds of steam from a severed pipe.

Ilfracombe, Monday 7th December 1914, with four Campbell paddle steamers at the pier - left to right
HMS *WESTWARD HO*, (Pendant No. 184); HMS *GLEN AVON*, (Pendant No. 185);
HMS *CAMBRIDGE*, (Pendant No. 183); HMS *LADY ISMAY*, (Pendant No. 186).

The ships called at Ilfracombe in order to replenish their water tanks on their much delayed journey from
Bristol to the east coast

AVEY & ARMY . MINE SWEEPERS & ARMY SERVICE CORPS   DEC 1914   Nº 4

The expanse of Ilfracombe pier made an ideal parade ground and was frequently used as such throughout the war. Here the men of the Army Service Corps are being put through their paces.

This, and the preceding three photographs, were taken by the Ilfracombe photographer, Gratton Phillipse. His caption for the above reads, "HM Minesweepers, (Late Campbell Pleasure Steamers)".

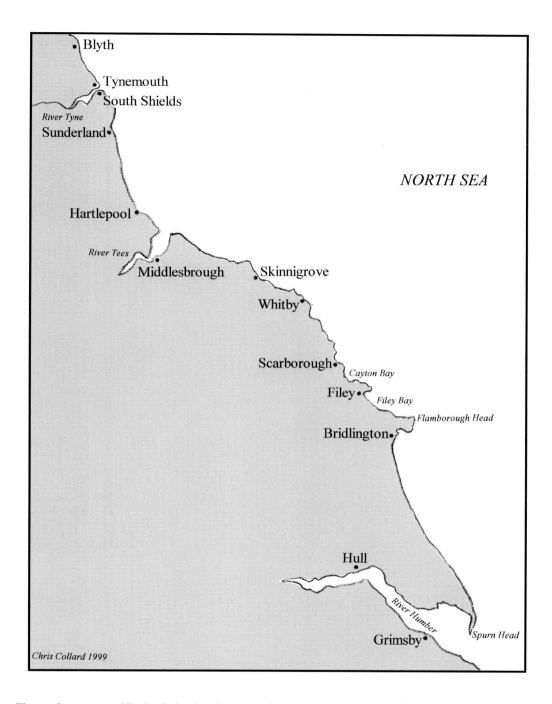

The north-east coast of England, showing the principal areas in which the Campbell minesweepers operated during the First World War.

P. & A. CAMPBELL, ꟾMITED.

DIRECTORS' REPORꞱ.

To be submitted at the Twenty Third Ordinary General Meeting to be held at the Grand Hotel, Bristol, on Monday, May 10th, 1915, at 3-30 p.m.

The Directors beg to present herewith a Summary of the Balance Sheet made up to the 31st day of December last, by which it will be seen that after payment of Interest on the Preference Shares at the rate of Six per cent. per annum and an Interim Dividend of two and a half per cent. (being at the rate of Five per cent. per annum) on the Ordinary Shares, there remains a balance of £18,374 13s. 9d. which the Directors propose to deal with as follows :—

	£	s.	d.
To Sinking Fund (raising same to £110,000)	10,000	0	0
„ Final Dividend of Seven and a half per cent. on Ordinary Shares (free of Income Tax) making Ten per cent. for the year.	3,750	0	0
„ Balance to carry forward	4,624	13	9
	£18,374	13	9

The New Steamer " Glen Usk," built by the Ailsa Shipbuilding Co., Ltd., and delivered in May last, was placed on the Newport Station, and has given complete satisfaction.

H.M. " Admiralty " have requisitioned Eight of the Steamers for Mine Sweeping, and H.M " War Office " have chartered P.S. " Barry " to act as Patrol in the upper reaches of the Bristol Channel.

The Directors hope that the Four remaining Steamers viz. " Ravenswood," " Waverley," " Glen Rosa," and " Albion," will be running at Whitsuntide.

Messrs. Ivie Mackie Dunlop and Peter Campbell retire by rotation and being eligible offer themselves for re-election.

Messrs. Ham, Dennehy & Co., the Auditors also retire and offer themselves for re-election.

IVIE M. DUNLOP, }

H. W. K. WAIT, } Directors.

B. W. CHRCHYARD, *Secretary.* ALEXANDER CAMPBELL,
April 30th, 1915. *Managing Director*

The P. & A. Campbell Directors Report for the year 1914.

The mines had been laid at a specific depth and as the tide ebbed, so their proximity to the surface of the water decreased, thereby increasing their danger to the deep-draught trawlers. There was little more that the flotilla could do under such circumstances, the skippers therefore took the safest course of action and dropped anchor.

Meanwhile, the *BRIGHTON QUEEN*, under the temporary command of Commander R. H. Walters, had been farther out in the North Sea on a sweeping exercise. She came in from seaward and joined the anchored flotilla in readiness to assist in the operation.

Later that afternoon, as the tide rose and rendered the mines less dangerous, the ships were on the move again and the trawlers continued with their sweeping. Lieut. Parsons reported to Capt. Massey-Dawson at Grimsby:

> "Proceeded this morning from Bridlington. Carried out sweep from one mile NE of Flamborough Head, passing close inside Filey Brig Buoy, to one mile SE of Scarborough Castle. While in this vicinity exploded 15 mines...Regret to report No. 99 struck mine and sank in ten minutes...Regret to report also that No. 58 struck a mine and is badly holed on the port bow. She is now being towed in by Brighton Queen: hope to beach her at Scarborough. Have received no communication from Commander Walters in BQ...In future no sweeps will take place anywhere in this section of coast except inside two hours of high water."

The *PASSING* was towed, stern first, across Cayton Bay and remained afloat just long enough for the *BRIGHTON QUEEN* to beach her on Scarborough Sands. She was salved and eventually rejoined her minesweeping consorts.

The sweeping of the Scarborough minefield continued throughout the bitterly cold weather and frequent gales of the winter with the Campbell minesweepers often augmenting a force of nearly thirty trawlers and drifters. The field accounted for the loss of nearly 100 lives and 20 vessels before it was completely cleared and declared safe for the passage of coastwise shipping in April 1915.

Apart from the laying of over 100 mines, the Scarborough raid was intended to serve another purpose. Admiral Von Ingenohl hoped that this further attack on coastal towns would induce the Admiralty to detach squadrons of the Grand Fleet and spread them along the coast, thus diminishing its overall fighting potential. However, Admiral Jellicoe had no intention of playing the German game. Apart from moving Rear-Admiral Beatty's battlecruiser squadron farther south to Rosyth, the Grand Fleet remained complete in Scapa Flow.

Scotland.

Submarine activity in the northern part of the North Sea led to fears for the safety of the Grand Fleet; Scapa Flow was unprotected against submarine attack. Although it was thought to be out of the question for any submerged vessel to penetrate the anchorage through the swirling currents of its rock studded channels, Admiral Jellicoe was of the opinion that it might just be possible for a submarine to get inside at slack water. In fact, an unconfirmed report of a periscope being sighted in the Flow on

Saturday 17th October caused considerable alarm and commotion, and the fleet was ordered to put to sea without delay. The installation of anti-submarine defences began immediately and pending their completion, the Grand Fleet was instructed to use anchorages around the coasts of Scotland and Northern Ireland. From HMS *LION*, anchored in Loch Na Keal, Isle of Mull, Rear-Admiral Beatty wrote to the First Lord :-

> "At present we feel that we are working up to a catastrophe of a very large character... All is not right somewhere... The menace of mines and submarines is proving larger every day. Adequate means to meet or combat them are not forthcoming and we are gradually being pushed out of the North Sea, and off our particular perch...."

The defences at Scapa Flow were hurried on with all speed, but on Tuesday 27th October, while the Grand Fleet was using Lough Swilly, in Northern Ireland, as a base for gunnery exercises, it suffered its first serious loss with the mining and subsequent sinking of the battleship, *AUDACIOUS*.

An extensive field of two hundred mines had been laid off Tory Island during the previous night by the North German Lloyd liner, *BERLIN*, her objective being the merchant traffic bound to and from Liverpool. This incident further emphasised the necessity for an extended and efficient minesweeping service, particularly as the White Star liner, *OLYMPIC*, crowded with passengers, had gone to the assistance of the *AUDACIOUS* and had run a grave risk of suffering the same fate.

The "catastrophe of a very large character", prophesied by Rear-Admiral Beatty, had occurred and proved without doubt that many more minesweepers were urgently required.

Minesweeping trawlers in the North Sea, 1914

A SEA OF TROUBLES

"It is doubtful if we could have defeated the enemy as quickly as we did if it had not been for the assistance which the Royal Navy received from the trawler patrol and the paddle minesweepers. Their officers and men showed great fortitude and a fine spirit by implicit obedience to orders, zeal and devotion to duty. No call was made to them without obtaining their most willing and ready response."

Admiral Sir Reginald Bacon.

"The Dover Patrol"

Scotland.

The *BRITANNIA* and the *GLEN USK* were requisitioned by the Admiralty on Wednesday 27th January 1915 and were destined to join the Grand Fleet minesweepers. The *BRITANNIA*, flagship of the White Funnel Fleet since entering service in 1896, was re-named *BRITAIN* in deference to the battleship, *BRITANNIA*, and was taken northward by one of the company's senior masters, Capt. Allan Livingstone. The *GLEN USK* was the company's most recent acquisition; a magnificent product of the Ailsa Shipbuilding Co. of Troon, which had entered service as recently as June 1914. For her journey north she was placed under the command of the Commodore of the Campbell fleet, Capt. Dan Taylor. On Friday 5th February 1915 they left Bristol for the River Clyde. Both vessels sailed at 08.45 and despite encountering gales in the Irish Sea, arrived at Harland & Wolff's yard, Glasgow, on the afternoon of Saturday 6th February 1915, where they were to be fitted out for their forthcoming duties.

Two months later their conversions had been completed and they were taken over by their naval personnel. The *GLEN USK*, (Pendant No. 189), was initially under the command of Lieut. Commander Gervase W. Heaton - the Flotilla Commander, and the *BRITAIN*, (Pendant No. 190), under Lieut. John A. Shuter. During early April they carried out practice sweeps with their consorts - the South Coast paddler, *BOURNEMOUTH QUEEN*, (renamed *BOURNE*); the North Wales paddler, *ST. ELVIES*; the Clyde paddle steamer *JUNO*, (renamed *JUNIOR*); and the *SLIEVE BEARNAGH*, one of the paddle steamers of the Belfast and County Down Railway Co.

Between sweeping practices they patrolled the Firth of Clyde on the lookout for submarines, covering from their bases at Troon and Ardrossan an area southward between Turnberry Head and Corsewall Point. On one such occasion the *GLEN USK* "grazed" a submerged rock near the island of Ailsa Craig. She sustained only slight damage - two plates were dented - but her log book notes that, on her return to Troon the Base Commander "admonished Lt. Commander Heaton to be more careful in future".

By mid-May the flotilla had begun sweeping in the Firth of Clyde but was then transferred to join the Grand Fleet in Northern Ireland, sailing from Troon to Moville,

41

Lough Foyle, on Wednesday 19th May 1915. Their duties continued without respite and on the following morning the *GLEN USK* and the *BOURNE* left their anchorage in the Lough, passed the island of Inishtrahull at 06.20, and began sweeping northwards. At 15.30 they were abeam of Barra Head, the southernmost point of the Outer Hebridean island of Berneray, where they turned and continued their sweep southward, arriving off Inishtrahull again at 02.50 on Friday 21st. After coaling at Londonderry later that morning, they set off for Berneray once more. These exceptionally long sweeps, which occupied the flotilla for three months, were made to protect the harbours of the west coast of Scotland, the northern approaches to the Clyde, and the harbours of the north-east coast of Ireland. They were interspersed with shorter sweeps between Inishtrahull and the Skerryvore Lighthouse, as well as similar operations in Lough Swilly and Sheep Haven for the protection of the various squadrons of the Grand Fleet. Moville, Buncrana and Londonderry were the ports in which they took on coal and supplies.

In August 1915 a considerable portion of the Grand Fleet was transferred to Invergordon, in the Cromarty Firth on Scotland's east coast, and Lieut. Commander Heaton's flotilla was detailed to accompany them. Whether the steamers proceeded in convoy or independently is not known; the only surviving log book recording the journey is that of the *GLEN USK*. She had been under repair at Troon but set off on the long haul around the north of Scotland on Saturday 21st August 1915:-

> "10.30   Left Troon for Cromarty.
> 13.10   Pladda abeam.
> 21.12   Dubh Artach lighthouse abeam.
>
> Sunday 22nd August 1915.
> 00.35   Skerryvore lighthouse abeam.
> 15.50   Cape Wrath abeam.
> 19.40   Anchored overnight in Thurso Bay.
>
> Monday 23rd August 1915.
> 04.45   Hove up and proceeded.
> 06.05   Duncansby Head.
> 19.40   Anchored in Buckie Roads.
>
> Tuesday 24th August 1915.
> 04.10   Up anchor and proceeded sweeping
>   with HMS Britain in the Moray Firth."

The first mining offensive against the Grand Fleet had taken place on the night of Friday 7th August 1915, when 380 mines were laid in the Moray Firth by the German auxiliary, *METEOR*. The sweepers were soon at work, including the *GLEN USK* and the *BRITAIN* which, as can be seen from the above log extract, began work as a matter of urgency on their arrival in the vicinity. A clear channel was swept along the northern side of the Moray Firth and over 200 mines were cleared from the southern side; those in the middle were left to form a defensive barrier. In a somewhat lighter vein, an officer involved in the sweeping of the minefield laid by the *METEOR*, stated that because of the depth at which the mines had been laid, sweeping was restricted to about 3½ hours either side of high water. During the periods when sweeping was not possible the flotilla anchored at various harbours along the coast of Elgin and Banffshire, such as Buckie, Banff and Lossiemouth, which provided a chance of landing officers and men for recreation. On its first visit to Banff, however, the flotilla incurred some unpopularity. The officer continues:-

> "We came in at dusk and anchored among various small buoys and floats. They were soon investigated and were found to be crab and lobster traps. Word was quickly passed around and you can imagine the result. Unfortunately we were discovered and, next morning, a deputation from Banff waited on our captain, with the result that anyone having crab or lobster was 'invited' to contribute to a fund making good the loss to the fishermen. I think they were the most expensive shellfish I have ever eaten!"

Improvements and modifications were constantly being made to German mines and their recovery for investigation was always desirable. The greater the knowledge of their operation, the better the minesweeping forces were able to keep one step ahead of the enemy. Their recovery was invariably a highly dangerous operation, as it was common knowledge that the only inefficient part of a German mine was the safety device intended to render it harmless.

In the course of sweeping in the Moray Firth, at 22.10 on Sunday 19th September 1915, a mine was swept up and buoyed in Cullen Bay. In order for it to be moved into shallow water for recovery and examination, two boats set off, one from the *GLEN USK* and the other from the *ST. ELVIES*. Their crews passed a wire and a long loop of chain around the mine; then, with considerable skill and great risk in the heavy swell, the mine, complete with its sinker, was cut adrift from its moorings and towed into Burghead Bay, where it was re-moored. The *GLEN USK* kept her searchlight on it throughout night and warned off approaching vessels. Next morning the mine was towed inshore by the same two boats, safely beached and rendered harmless. Lieut. Commander Heaton reported on the magnificent work of the individual boats' crews to Admiral Jellicoe, and among those ratings specially commended were Patrick Welsh and Amos Martin of the *GLEN USK*. Both were "Campbell men", and it was Pat Welsh who carried out the difficult and dangerous task of removing the clockwork mechanism of the salvaged mine. Also commended were J. T. Williams and Bezeleel Jones of the *ST. ELVIES*. With regard to the latter Lieut. Commander Heaton added, "This man is always more than ready and willing to undertake any extra work which may come along, however difficult, and was coxswain of a boat employed in salving German mine and sinker No. 6842..."

Admiral Jellicoe, in turn, wrote to the Admiralty on 22nd September 1915, "A complete mine and sinker has been recovered intact... under circumstances reflecting much credit to those concerned. The mine, which contained 290lbs. of wet guncotton, has been unloaded and is at Scapa Flow. It is proposed to use it for trials with the Usborne Kite Mine Defence System." He also commented on the "pluck, ingenuity and good seamanship" of those involved. In fact, Admiral Jellicoe paid a visit to the *BRITAIN* some time later to express, in person, his appreciation of the work which the flotilla was doing.

C O N F I D E N T I A L.

Admiralty,
13th February, 1915.

(stamp: COMMANDER IN CHIEF / 14 FEB 1915 / HOME FLEETS)

Commander-in-Chief,
Home Fleets.

    Submitted. The following paddle steamers have been taken up for mine sweeping service in the Clyde:-

Ship.	Length.	Draught loaded.	Speed.	Where fitting out.	Date to complete fitting out.
"JUNIOR" ("June")	245 ft.	6' 9".	19 kts.	Clyde.	20 Feb.15.
"GLEN USK". ("Glen Usk")	224 ft.	6' 0".	Probably about 17½ knots	Clyde.	27 Feb.15.
"BRITAIN" ("Britannia").	230 ft.	6' 6".	20 kts.	Clyde.	6 Mch.15.
"BOURNE". ("Bournemouth Queen").	200 ft.	5' 6".	16 kts.	Southampton.	Not yet reported.

    The following ships are being surveyed as regards machinery and boilers. If found satisfactory they will also be taken up for Clyde service:-

"EAGLE III"	215 ft.	5' 6".	16 kts.
"SLIEVE BERNAGH".	225 ft.	5' 3".	17 kts.

    As the supply of 12-pdr. guns is low at present, only one 12-pdr. gun will be mounted in these vessels for the time being.

    Alterations are being carried out to provide sufficient coal and water stowage to permit of the vessels remaining at sea at 14 knots for three days.

    These vessels will be tenders to "PACTOLUS".

    A copy of this has been sent to Admiral, Rosyth.

A memo from Rear-Admiral Edward Charlton to Admiral Jellicoe informing him of the requisition of six paddle steamers. The expected date of completion of their fitting out was somewhat over-optimistic.

PRO Ref: ADM137/1886

The photographer's subject was, no doubt, the steam yacht in this view of Troon harbour; but it is the background which is of particular relevance to our story. On the right is HMS *GLEN USK*; on the left, the bow of HMS *JUNIOR*; and just visible alongside the cargo vessel in the centre is HMS *BOURNE*. The photograph was probably taken in April or May 1915, shortly after Lieut. Commander Heaton's flotilla had completed refitting and were assembling at Troon prior to commencing their patrol duties in the Firth of Clyde. The bridge, and the deckhouses of the *GLEN USK* and *JUNIOR* still retain their varnished teak finish and are not yet painted in warship grey.

H.M.S. " Glen Usk " , Thursday 16th day of April , 1918 .

From , To , or At At Sea

15

Hours	Patent Log	Distance Run		Standard Compass Courses	Deviation of Standard Compass	Revolutions per minute	Wind		Weather	State of the Sea	Height of Barometer and Attached Thermometer	Temperature			Position			REMARKS	Initials of the Officer of the Watch
		Miles	Tenths				Direction	Force				Air	Wet Bulb	Sea	8.0 a.m.	8.0 p.m.			
															Position	Latitude	Longitude	A.M.	
1																		Patrolling as for 15th inst	
2							SW												
3																			
4								2	Dull		30·1							4.0	
5									Clear									Patrolling as required	
6																		7.25 Cornwall Pt. S.55°W. Ailsa Craig N30′ [E]	
7																		7.28 A.M. Stopped Engines	
8							NW	2	Clear		30·1							7.30 Stopped Engines 7.31 Half Speed Ahead	
9																		8.0 Mod. "Pernette"	
10																		8.10 A.M. weather bottom	
11																		Clear with decks	

PRO Ref: ADM53/42956

	Variation	True Bearing and Distance	Currents in the 24 hours ending at Noon	D.R. Obs.		D.R. Obs.	P.M.	Fresh Meat	Vegetables	Bread	Received Distilled Expended Remaining	Coal Oil	Coal Oil	Expended for all purposes
1							1.0 Pd Ship's hands Mabo						
2							to K's and Quarters						
3													
4				20. 2 Glen 30.2			3.30. Clear of boats.						
5							4.10 Condr "Christian" came onboard 25						9.9
6							6 leave to Star Watch & Fife 16.30 pm						
7													
8				21. 2 Ditto 30.3			8.0				0			
9													
10													
11													
12													

8.—3214.

The log of the GLEN USK for Thursday 15th April 1915; the day on which she made contact with a rock near Ailsa Craig.

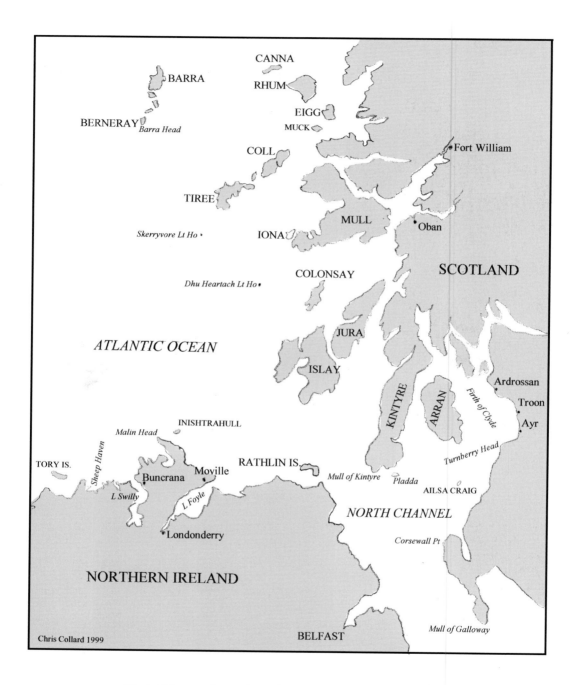

The initial areas of operations of Lieut. Commander Heaton's flotilla.

HMS *GLEN USK*, (right) and HMS *BRITAIN*, (left), in the early months of their naval service.

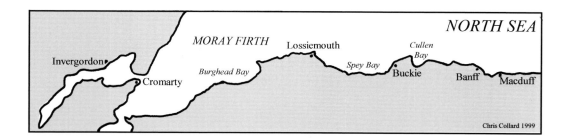

The Moray Firth.

H.M.S. " Glen Usk " , Sun 19 th day of September , 1915.

From Cromarty , To Sea , or At

Hours	Patent Log Miles	Patent Log Tenths	Standard Compass Courses	Deviation of Standard Compass	Revolutions per minute	Wind Direction	Wind Force	Weather	State of the Sea	Height of Barometer and Attached Thermometer	Temperature Air	Temperature Wet Bulb	Temperature Sea	REMARKS
														Position 8.0 a.m. · Latitude · Longitude
														8.0 p.m. ·
														A.M.
1														
2														
3														
4														4.20 called over Stokers cable
5														5.15 weighed anchor. 5.45 passed outer boom defence Co S80E. 5.30 full speed
6														
7														7.15 transferred wheels to Britain. 7.58 Covesea Lt abeam 5/8 S65E. Set Log
8						E S E	misty wet			30.25				
9														9.21 ¾ Port Knockie log 15¾ miles
10														10.10 Anchored in Cullen Bay to assist St Elvies in saving mines sinker

Fuel .

	Expended for all purposes	Tons
	Coal	
	Oil	
	Remaining	Tons
	Coal	
	Oil	

Fresh Water

		Tons
	Received	
	Distilled	
	Expended	
	Remaining	

Provisions Received

		lbs.
	Fresh Meat	
	Vegetables	
	Bread	

Number on Sick List

	D.R.	
	Obs.	

Longitude

	D.R.	
	Obs.	

Currents in the 24 hours ending at Noon

Variation

True Bearing and Distance

P.M.

3.25 weighed anchor. & escort St Elmo in towing mine to Burghead Bay.

10.0 Anchored in Burghead Bay kep watch over mine during the night

1			
2			
3	S E fresh	30 24	
4			
5			
6			
7	" "	30 23	
8			
9			
10			
11			

The log of the GLEN USK for Sunday 19th September 1915; which gives the very briefest of details concerning the salving of a German mine and its sinker.
PRO Ref: ADM53/42958

Among the surviving records of minesweeping operations are two reports from Lieut. Commander Heaton to Admiral Jellicoe outlining the activities of the ships and personnel under his command. They provide a compelling insight into the day to day problems which confronted the Flotilla Commander, and are quoted here in slightly edited form. His report of 5th October 1915, from the *ST. ELVIES*, then at Macduff, states:-

"In connection with the work of this flotilla since its formation in February, and in particular with the sweeping operations just completed in the Moray Firth, which occupied from 15th August to 5th October inclusive, during which period the flotilla destroyed 74 mines, (71 moored and 3 floating), I have the honour to report as follows:-

1. From 26th to 30th September inclusive, the flotilla was in harbour, weatherbound. Otherwise it has been at sea for the first three weeks, when not coaling from colliers, (frequently unassisted by outside labour), on average under way 16 hours per day. From then on, in order to keep the ships running, the flotilla has been organised so as to have four ships sweeping while two ships complete with coal, stores, etc.

2. During these operations all the ships have been severely shaken by mine explosions in sweeps, and portions of mines have frequently alighted on their decks. Several men have received minor injuries but nothing serious; the conduct of all concerned has been exemplary.

3. I consider that the greatest credit is due to the engine room staffs of all the ships for the satisfactory manner in which they have kept these vessels running, especially when one considers that on their previous service, before being taken over by the Admiralty, the engineers had little to do but run the engines, all defects being taken in hand as they developed by specialised overseers and workmen from shore. Practically all of these vessels are very old and were never intended for this continued steaming.

4. I have the honour to especially bring to your notice the following officers and men:- Lieut. John A. Shuter, RN. This officer has been in command of the "Junior" and "Britain" since the beginning of July 1915 and by his efforts and loyalty has greatly increased their efficiency. Lieut. A. H. Chafer, RNR. This officer, I understand, commenced minesweeping on 17th September 1914, as section leader of 6 boats of the Humber Trawler Flotilla, and at one period last winter spent 5 weeks on the minefields off the Yorkshire coast. He remained in that command until the middle of July 1915, since when he has most ably commanded the "Bourne" and "Slieve Bearnagh". Temp. Lieut William Highton, RNR. Ever since his ship - the "St. Elvies", joined the flotilla this officer has been more than zealous to learn this new work. His ship was trained to sweep in two days; he is always ready and has a practically clean Defaulters Sheet as a consequence of his untiring efforts. His bearing on the minefields has been exemplary, and the successful salving operations of German mine and sinker No. 6842, which occupied almost the whole of September 19th and 20th, were mainly due to his magnificent conduct, resource and endeavour.

Temp. Assistant Engineer J. W. Davies, RNR. This officer was seriously considering retiring from active employment, but when his ship, the "St. Elvies", was taken over by the Government he immediately volunteered his services. These have been of the greatest value in the ship and his knowledge and experience has, at all times, been at the disposal of all the ships in the flotilla.

Temp. Assistant Engineer A. E. Jenkins, RNR. HMS Glen Usk. In addition to the extremely satisfactory manner in which the machinery of this ship has been kept, this officer is always ready for any writing or additional work, and the practically total absence of Defaulters in his vessel may be attributed largely to his influence."

Lieut. Commander Heaton also mentioned Temp. Sub-Lieut. Angus Morrison, RNR., for his untiring efforts in the running of the *SLIEVE BEARNAGH*, which he found that, "through age and previous neglect is easily the worst ship in the flotilla".

A further report was issued on 5th December 1915 which included the following items:-

"On 6th October we were ordered to sweep the southern shore of the Moray Firth. We continued doing this until 11th October, when all six vessels, (being long overdue for boiler scaling and all having more or less urgent defects), were detailed by the Captain, Minesweepers to get fit. In accordance with this order the ships were laid up at Invergordon from 14th to 22nd October, being patched up to run for a few weeks longer.

Meanwhile, on 11th October, an oil steamer damaged "Britain's" bows while she was lying at anchor off Invergordon. She was accordingly dispatched to Aberdeen on 13th October for dry-docking and, at the same time, to get all other defects made good....

During operations which were carried out by four vessels from 23rd October to 17th November, I took the opportunity to get "Britain", "Glen Usk", and "St. Elvies" thoroughly overhauled at Aberdeen. W/T was transferred from "Glen Usk" to "St. Elvies", in which ship, with the new operators, it has been quite satisfactory....

I had also arranged for "Junior" to follow "St. Elvies" at Aberdeen, but as the largest of her defects consisted of new condensor doors, I suggested to the Engineer Captain at Invergordon that if these could be ordered from her builders, valuable time might be saved over her refit. This accordingly has been done, but as their delivery cannot be made before the middle of December, and as the "Junior" is still able to run, arrangements have been made for her to be taken in hand at Aberdeen on 20th December and Admiral, Rosyth, has been asked to send a relief for her if possible.

"Bourne" and "Slieve Bearnagh", which all along have been a continual drag on the remainder, their sweeping speed at best being no more than 7.5 knots of late, have now reached the stage where it would be dangerous for them to run any longer without an overhaul of approximately six weeks. They are no longer efficient enough to risk the long run to and from Cromarty, so often required by the rapid change of weather conditions in the Moray Firth. Arrangements for their overhaul with Admiral, Rosyth, are in the course of negotiation, and are briefly that they will be sent to Glasgow, or elsewhere, for an extensive refit, their crews being turned over to two more suitable vessels if possible, to again rejoin this unit with which they have been trained to work.

In addition a seventh paddler has been asked for... Seven paddlers would allow for the most economical and efficient working - one pair in harbour, two pairs out and one vessel refitting and scaling boilers. With less than this number, one vessel laid up necessarily lays up a pair.... In spite of the most inclement weather, and nights spent at anchor with the ships rolling heavily and creaking in every joint, the conduct of the crews of all vessels has been exemplary.

I have the honour to be, Sir,
Your obedient servant,
Gervase W. H. Heaton
Acting Commander, Senior Officer Paddle Minesweepers,(N.E.Coast)."

The submarine defences at Scapa Flow were completed towards the end of 1915 and the ships of the Grand Fleet began to return. However, many of those which had been moved to Rosyth in late 1914, including Rear Admiral Beatty's battlecruisers, remained in the Firth of Forth, and it was in this area that the *BRITAIN* and the *GLEN USK* were to spend the rest of the war.

Orders were issued by Admiral Jellicoe to Lieut. Commander Heaton on 18th December 1915 which stated:-

"...Rear Admiral, Invergordon, has been directed to despatch the six paddle minesweepers for thorough refits and overhauls as follows:-
"Bourne" and "Slieve Bearnagh" to the Clyde.
"Junior" to Aberdeen p.m. Monday 20th December.
"St. Elvies","Glen Usk" and "Britain" to Leith on Tuesday 21st December.
The "Bourne" and "Slieve Bearnagh" will probably be six or eight weeks refitting, the remainder three weeks. Directions have been given to the vessels to proceed to Leith on completion of their refits.

The Grimsby Paddlers.

New Year's Day 1915 found five ships of the flotilla sheltering from storms in Middlesbrough; the exception was the *DEVONIA* which was in dock at Hull with cylinder trouble. The steamers had been hard at work on the east coast, clearing the Scarborough minefield which had blocked the War Channel to the north of Grimsby. They were then sent to the Thames estuary and operated from Sheerness on the Isle of Sheppey before making their way north again to Harwich, Lowestoft and Great Yarmouth in mid-February.

The notable yachtsman, G. H. P. Muhlhauser, was serving, at that time, in the requisitioned steam yacht, *SAGITTA*. She had been converted for minesweeping and worked with the Campbell paddlers on many occasions during the early part of the war.

In his book, "Small Craft", Lieut. Muhlhauser states:-

> "We were suddenly ordered away from Harwich to the vicinity of Beachy Head; several ships had been lost there and mines were suspected. Quite a crowd of us, including the Campbell paddlers from Grimsby, spent a couple of days searching the area without finding anything in the way of mines and it was finally decided that the lost ships must have been torpedoed."

During the course of this operation, on Friday 26th February, the *WESTWARD HO* and the *GLEN AVON* berthed at Eastbourne Pier to take on water. Although those particular vessels had never visited the Sussex coast in peacetime, their call was, nevertheless, a poignant reminder of happier days in bygone years.

After their brief sortie off Beachy Head the flotilla returned to the east coast.

The ships were pushed to their limits, consequently, accidents and breakdowns were not uncommon. As an example, the following list itemises necessary repairs for a two month period in 1915:-

Tuesday 12th January.	
DEVONIA	New cylinder fitted at Earl's Yard, Hull.
Friday 22nd January.	
CAMBRIDGE.	Received damage to five plates in port bow and quarter while crossing HMS *DUNCAN* in the Thames. Went into dry dock at Sheerness.
Friday 5th February.	
LADY ISMAY.	At Grimsby. Re-bushing pins in paddle wheels.
Monday 15th February.	
CAMBRIDGE.	At Grimsby. Repairing broken paddle arm.
Monday 22nd February.	
DEVONIA. *LADY ISMAY.* }	At Sheerness for unspecified repairs.
Friday 26th February.	
BRIGHTON QUEEN.	Sailed from off Eastbourne to have bow damage repaired at Southampton.
Saturday 27th February.	
WESTWARD HO.	Left Dover for Sheerness for stem repair - damaged by *GLEN AVON* that morning.

The monotony of their day to day minesweeping was occasionally relieved by moments of "excitement" such as that which occurred on Tuesday 28th April 1915. The *WESTWARD HO* was sweeping with the *SAGITTA*, when two mines exploded in their sweep. Lieut. Muhlhauser was aboard the armed yacht and stated that in the silence after the explosion, as the two ships lay rolling to the disturbance of the water, a third mine bobbed to the surface. The *SAGITTA'S* commander, Lieut. W. H. S. Garnett, RNR., jumped overboard, swam to the mine, cut the two external wires leading to the

HMS *WESTWARD HO* early in 1915, with her crew hauling in the kite

HMS *BRITAIN* in 1915

detonator, and secured a line around it. It was then hoisted on board and brought into harbour in triumph. Lieut. Garnett took a considerable risk in his action but, as with the Moray Firth operation, the recovery of the mine for research was of great importance.

In order to ensure that mariners reported sightings of suspicious vessels and stray mines, a system of "rewards" was instituted. Admiralty Monthly Orders No. 64 of 1915 provided for payments to be made for "the proven destruction of enemy mines in certain areas." Article 2 of the monthly orders defined the "certain areas" as those only in which navigation was permitted, ie. outside the marked danger areas. However, a further restriction was imposed specifically on the minesweepers which stated that rewards were not payable when they were "...under orders from the Admiralty to navigate in those regions and clear the minefields." Therefore their payments were limited to any "rogue" mines which they came across on passage to and from their designated areas. For each mine so destroyed an amount of £5 0s 0d. would be payable per vessel and distributed to her personnel by way of a share system. The sweeping of stray mines proved to be a lucrative business as a letter from Admiral Charlton to the Admiralty, reproduced on page 59 shows.

A skirmish between the White Funnel steamers and a U-boat occurred on the afternoon of Saturday 14th August 1915, when the *BRIGHTON QUEEN, WESTWARD HO, GLEN AVON* and *CAMBRIDGE* were sweeping near Smith's Knoll. Some U-boats had been shadowing a number of Lowestoft smacks which were fishing near the sweepers and at 14.15 a submarine was spotted heading for the fishing craft. Immediately the steamers slipped their sweeps and made for the intruder at full speed, opening fire with their small guns. The *BRIGHTON QUEEN* claimed to have scored a hit on the enemy's conning tower but it could not positively be verified. The submarine, subsequently confirmed to have been UB4, dived and made off, only to be sunk later that evening by the gallant action of the crew of the armed fishing ketch, *INVERLYON.*

The question of U-boat operations had been the cause of much argument between the German Naval Command and the German politicians since the outbreak of the war. The torpedoing of the Cunard liner, *LUSITANIA*, off the Old Head of Kinsale, in Southern Ireland in May 1915 with the loss of 1198 passengers and the sinking of the British liner, *ARABIC*, on 19th August 1915 in the same vicinity, with the loss of 44 passengers, drew such strong protestations from America and Great Britain that the U-boat commanders were placed under severe constraints which effectively ended the campaign for the rest of the year.

The Dover Patrol.

The Dover Patrol, under the overall command of Admiral Sir Reginald Bacon, blocked the southern exit from the North Sea. The demands of naval strategy as a whole meant that the resources allocated to it were limited. The ubiquitous trawlers and drifters had been stationed there since the beginning of the war and were performing sterling work by patrolling and maintaining the nets which they had laid in order to trap any German U-boats which might venture into the English Channel.

Admiral Bacon, like all of his counterparts, had nothing but praise for the crews who manned the fishing craft, but, again like his counterparts, had a favourite tale to tell. He recounted that a member of the crew of a trawler was suffering from a serious attack of rheumatism and a civilian doctor ordered him to hospital. Before leaving the trawler the doctor instructed the skipper to signal the information to his base and to have an ambulance sent for the man so that he could meet his patient at the hospital on arrival. The man did not arrive at the hospital at the appointed time and eventually the irate doctor re-visited the trawler to ascertain the reason for the man's absence.

The skipper informed him, "Well, we tried to send him ashore but a police sergeant hailed us and told us that on no account was he to be landed or we'd be fined a hundred pounds, so we kept him aboard". "But didn't you signal to your base and tell them it was only a case of rheumatism", said the mystified doctor. "Yes we did", replied the skipper, "but neither me nor the signalman could spell rheumatism so we called it small-pox instead".

Until June 1915, all enemy minefields had been laid by surface ships, but in that month came a most unwelcome development with the advent of submarine minelayers. Two new types of small submarine were under construction in German shipyards: the coastal "UB" boats of about 130 tons surface displacement, which carried a pair of torpedo tubes, and the "UC's", about 40 tons larger, which carried twelve mines fitted in vertical tubes built into the hull. The UCs were the earliest submarine minelayers and proved to be a considerable thorn in the flesh.

This new method of minelaying threw a very heavy strain on the minesweeping forces at Harwich, The Nore and Dover, which were the first areas to be affected. In spite of the increasing size of the minesweeping force, it was barely able to meet the demands put upon it by the increased intensity of the German minelaying offensive.

The Dover area had been relatively immune to the surface minelayers but received its fair share of attention with the advent of the UCs from mid-1915. The trawler fleet, which now had to contend with minesweeping in addition to its patrolling duties, was considerably overstretched and was very soon supplemented by a flotilla of hired paddle steamers. The paddlers were placed under the command of the Port Minesweeping Officer, Commander Walter G. Rigg RN.

The *RAVENSWOOD*, (Pendant No. 588), and the *ALBION* were the next White Funnel steamers to be commissioned; the latter being re-named *ALBYN*, (Pendant No. 587), to avoid confusion with the battleship *ALBION*. After conversion at Bristol they left the Floating Harbour on the morning of Thursday 1st July 1915 and called at Minehead pier, where their naval commanders, Lieut. Arthur Sanders, (ex *BRIGHTON QUEEN*), and Sub-Lieut. Ben Whitehead, took over from Capts. Ashford and Denman, who disembarked after acting as pilots. The steamers took on water at Eastbourne pier on the following afternoon and arrived at Dover on Saturday 3rd July.

By the middle of the month they had been joined by three Clyde paddle steamers: *MARMION* and *JUPITER*, (both of which received the suffix "II" added to their names to avoid confusion with other vessels), and the *DUCHESS OF MONTROSE*; the South Coast paddler, *BALMORAL*, completed the flotilla. At Dover they took their places in the severely congested harbour, crammed with every kind of vessel from the large monitors and cruisers to submarines and coastal motor-boats. Admiral Bacon described the ships of the Dover Patrol as "The Miscellaneous Fleet" - 400 vessels of 24 different types.

On 29th July 1915 the *ALBYN* and *JUPITER II*, came across their first minefield near the South Goodwin Sands. Two mines came to the surface in their sweep and the entire

Admiralty,
16th June 1915.

Issued, dated 9 July 1915.

With reference to the attached lists of mines
destroyed, I approve of payment being made at the rate of £5
per mine, as follows:--

Ship to pay.	Vessels to be paid.	Amount to be paid.	Estmtd.apprx value of 'one' share
HALCYON	Daimler, Desiree	£25.00.00.	£0-16-8.
SAGITTA	Sagitta	£3. 6. 8.)	£0- 1-2.
PEKIN	Lady Ismay, Westward Ho, Brighton Queen	£6.13. 4.)	
SAGITTA	Sagitta	£21-15-0.)	
PEKIN	Devonia, Lady Ismay, Cambridge, Westward Ho, Brighton Queen, Loyal Prince	£78. 2. 0.)	£0. 7. 3.
HALCYON	Daimler, Desiree, Whooper, Volante, Sargon, North King II, Unitia, Eager, Furze, Kent County	£50. 3. 0.)	
PEKIN	Devonia, Cambridge, Glen Avon, Westward Ho	£215. 0. 0.	£1. 6.10.
PEKIN	Devonia, Lady Ismay, Cambridge, Westward Ho, Brighton Queen, Glen Avon, Recepto, R.Irvin, Lord Durham, Cuirass	£420. 0. 0.	£1. 8. 0.
SAGITTA	Sagitta	£49. 0. 0.)	£0.16. 4.
PEKIN	Devonia, Lady Ismay, Cambridge, Brighton Queen, Glen Avon, Recepto, Cuirass & '852'	£201. 0. 0.)	
PEKIN	Westward Ho, & '852	£5. 0. 0.	£0. 1.10.
PEKIN	Devonia, Brighton Queen	£5. 0. 0.	£0. 1. 3.
SAGITTA	Sagitta	£17.12. 0.)	£0. 5.10.
PEKIN	Lady Ismay, Cambridge, Westward Ho, Brighton Queen, Recepto & '852'	£55.18. 0.)	
HALCYON	Eager, Kent County	£6.10. 0.)	

2.   The money is to be distributed by shares, giving

2 shares to each Officer.
1½ shares to P.O's and C.P.O's.
1 share to ratings below P.O.

A memo issued by Rear-Admiral Charlton authorising the payment of rewards to the personnel of those ships which had swept up stray mines. The "Ship to Pay" column refers to the shore base under whose orders the flotillas acted.

PRO Ref: ADM137/1067

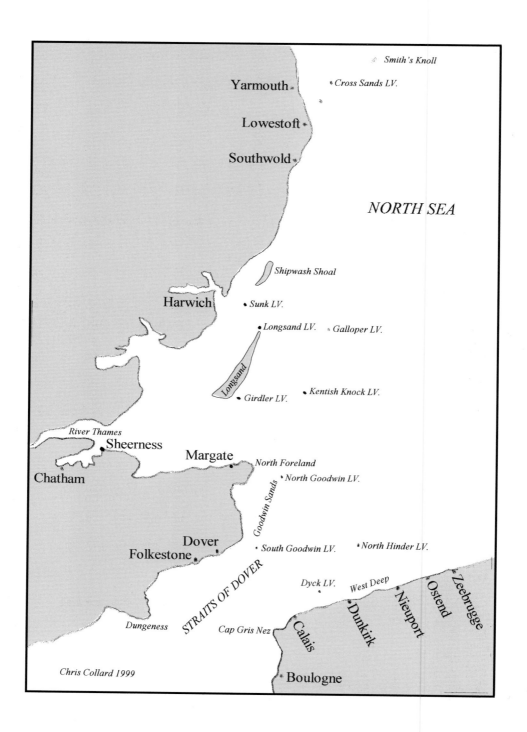

Smith's Knoll

Cross Sands LV.

Yarmouth

Lowestoft

Southwold

NORTH SEA

Shipwash Shoal

Harwich

Sunk LV.

Longsand LV.

Galloper LV.

Longsand

Kentish Knock LV.

Girdler LV.

River Thames

Sheerness

Margate

North Foreland

North Goodwin LV.

Chatham

Goodwin Sands

Dover

South Goodwin LV.

North Hinder LV.

Folkestone

Dyck LV.

West Deep

Ostend

Zeebrugge

Nieuport

Dunkirk

STRAITS OF DOVER

Dungeness

Cap Gris Nez

Calais

Boulogne

Chris Collard 1999

South-east England and the coasts of France and Belgium. (Not all lightvessels in the area are shown)

HMS *RAVENSWOOD* in the Straits of Dover.

HMS *RAVENSWOOD* with her port paddle box damaged, moored to a buoy at an unknown location.

191 5. **From** ⟨illegible⟩ **to** ⟨illegible⟩ **, or at** Dover ⟨illegible⟩

REMARKS	Initials of the Officer of the Watch

5.0 Hove up anchor and proceeded to sea in company
with H.M.S Marmion. Ravenswood + Montrose.
Sweeping + manoeuvring carried out off Dover
7.15. Slipped + proceeded to Dover.
8.0 Let go Port anchor veared 30 fthms Cable.
9.30 Filled tanks from water boat. Scrubbed + Washed Decks
Hands variously employed

	Noon.		
Latitude		Longitude	
	° ′		° ′
D.R.		D.R.	
Obs.		Obs.	

1.0 W. Middelton Deck Hand Left ship for Hospital
Hands variously employed

2.0 Cleared up decks

No Leave Granted

Lights Out Piped down

Log of HMS *ALBYN* for Thursday 12th August 1915.

PRO Ref: ADM53/33257

ships' companies, most of whom were as yet unfamiliar with them, gathered on deck to "watch the fun" while they were sunk by rifle fire. One of the shots hit a horn and the mine exploded. They had expected "a bit of a bang" but the explosion was so terrific that half of them fell down the hatchways, much to the amusement of those who had managed to stay on their feet!

The same two vessels were soon involved in an incident of a more gruesome nature. A report of the Commanding Officer of the *JUPITER II* states:-

> "...Near the Dyck Lightvessel a heavy explosion occurred. The French fishing smack 'Charles' of Gravelines had been blown up by a mine. We picked up two men - one dead, one living. We worked on the latter for two hours but he was too far gone and died on board. Albyn picked up one body; there was another visible with his head blown off, but sank before we reached him."

The horrifying realities of the job were learned all too quickly. Nevertheless, under the watchful eye and vigorous supervision of Commander Rigg, the personnel of the Dover Paddlers rapidly gained experience and expertise; qualities which were soon to be tested to their utmost!

The advance of the German land forces into Belgium lead to the fall of Antwerp on 9th October 1914. This released a large number of troops who immediately advanced to the coast and captured the seaports of Zeebrugge and Ostend, paving the way for the establishment of warship bases and attendant shore batteries. Early in 1915 consideration had been given to the destruction of those installations by monitors: the large, slow and somewhat cumbersome warships whose primary function was long range bombardment with their massive guns. Initially three monitors were detailed for the operations, each equipped with 12in guns with a range of nearly 12 miles. The number and size of the German shore batteries was not known, but their armament was believed to be a total of about forty guns ranging from 7ins to 11ins. At that stage of the war there was no reliable method of ascertaining the accuracy of long range, ship to shore bombardment. Eventually the solution was found: manned observation stations were to be placed between the monitors and the shore, each station wide of the direction of the ships' fire. The observers would locate the fall of the shells by way of instruments and relay this information, by signal lamp, to the gunnery officers aboard the monitors, thus enabling them to make necessary calculations and adjustments to the direction or inclination of their fire.

Each of the observation stations, known as a tripods, consisted of a tapering, three-sided framework constructed from railway lines. Their bases formed equilateral triangles with 23ft sides; their height was 40ft and the apex of the structure was surmounted by the observers' platform which measured about 6ft by 5ft. They were stowed on the decks of small cargo vessels which carried them to their positions and lowered them into the sea by way of their derricks, with their crews of two observers, two signalmen and instruments already "on board"! One can only marvel at the fortitude of those men who must have possessed the proverbial "nerves of steel".

By August 1915 the planning and preparations for the bombardment of the Belgian coast had been completed and the first operation was to take place on 21st of that month. The forces involved consisted of the three monitors which carried out the actual bombardment; nine destroyers which provided a screen of anti-submarine patrols between the ships and the shore; two tripod ships, each carrying an observation station, and each with a drifter in tow to rescue the observers if necessary during the firing; and a fleet of about eighty drifters to run a zareba of nets around the monitors in case of a seaward submarine attack.

The whole fleet was to be preceded on both the outward and homeward crossings by a flotilla of minesweepers consisting of the Dover Paddlers, and five of the six Grimsby Paddlers which had been deployed for the purpose. (The exception was the *DEVONIA*, which was undergoing replacement of boiler tubes in Grimsby).

Units of the fleet assembled at a variety of ports on the east coast and their times of sailing were arranged so that all of them should meet in the vicinity of the Galloper Lightvessel just before dark on 21st August. The rendezvous was accomplished successfully but there was an extremely heavy sea running; the two tripod ships with their observation platforms on board were particularly vulnerable and the operation was postponed. The fleet was dispersed at dawn on 22nd August with orders to reassemble that night.

Shortly after daybreak, as the paddlers were making their way towards Dover, the commander of the *ALBYN* sighted an enemy seaplane making straight for his ship. Sub-Lieut. Alexander Daniels immediately set the vessel on a zig-zag course at full speed. He judged the moment when he thought that the seaplane was about to drop a bomb and put the engines full astern. The ship had barely lost way when three bombs fell close ahead. The German pilot made another similar attempt but Sub-Lieut. Daniels repeated his manoeuvre. This time four bombs were dropped, the nearest missing by twenty yards. The seaplane made off, its pilot disgusted at this exemplary display of paddle steamer manoeuvrability!

Later that day the Belgian coast forces left their bases and re-assembled for their assault on the enemy positions in Zeebrugge. The following account is taken from the report submitted to the Vice-Admiral of the Dover Patrol by Commander Rigg:-

> 'I left Dover at 15.50 on 22nd August 1915 with the paddle minesweepers Marmion II, (Lt. Hubert B. Boothby DSO. RNR.); Albyn, (Sub-Lt. Alexander Daniels RNR.); Duchess of Montrose, (Lt. Alexander Duff Thomson RNR.); Ravenswood, (Lt. William Ellis RNR. of PMS Balmoral); and Jupiter II, (Lt. George Phipps Spooner RNR.), which vessel worked under the orders of Commander R. H. Walters with five of the Grimsby paddlers.
>
> I proceeded in accordance with your orders to a position five miles SE of the North Hinder Lightvessel, arriving there at 22.35. I waited there until midnight and then carried out sweeping to a position NE with as broad a front as possible. At 03.25 on 23 August I took station ahead of the destroyer Amazon and then acted under her commander's instructions until observation station No. 2 was laid when I turned and swept backwards and forwards until the return journey commenced.'

Similar procedures had been followed with the other observation station and both were now safely in position. The drifters had surrounded the monitors with nets and the bombardment began. Almost immediately the German batteries returned fire but the shells fell short of their targets. The tripods, however, were within range but remained unseen by the enemy throughout the whole operation. The observers transmitted their vital information to the monitors with an almost complete disregard for the missiles flying past them from both sides!

Shortly after 08.00 the bombardment ceased and the ships, all of which had escaped damage, prepared for the return crossing. No submarine activity had been seen during the action but as a precaution the paddlers again swept before the fleet. Commander Rigg's report continues:-

> "No hostile mines were discovered but on the return journey a British mine was swept up. It was sunk by the destroyer, Nubian.
>
> The following remarks are submitted - When minesweepers are waiting at night for the squadron they are to sweep ahead of, some recognition signal between the minesweepers and the squadron should be arranged. This will then enable the officer in charge of sweepers to get his sweeps out when the squadron arrives at the appointed place. While I waited in my allocated position several destroyers arrived at different times and owing to the darkness I was unable to distinguish whether they were the Amazon or not. Consequently, when Amazon did arrive it was a few minutes before I actually got ahead with my sweeps."

The operation was deemed to have been a success: intelligence received from Belgium, and reports from aircraft during the course of the ensuing weeks indicated that the damage inflicted on the military installations, while not exceptionally severe, was sufficient to convince Admiral Bacon that such actions should continue.

The second operation took place in September 1915 and followed similar proceedures. This time, however, the enemy was better prepared. Commander Rigg stated that on arriving off the Belgian coast on the morning of 25th September, the paddlers retired to a position astern of the monitors, within the drifters' nets, and were spread at large intervals to minimise the risk from hostile aircraft which persistently dropped bombs in close proximity, although without success, during the operation. He added:-

> "I would point out that the paddle minesweepers are an extremely good target for aircraft owing to the large expanse of their upper decks, and on all occasions of air attack the paddlers were made the object of specific attention."

The raids continued at regular intervals with refinements and improvements of strategy constantly being implemented. Nearly thirty such operations were carried out during the course of the war which eventually led to the enemy's abandonment of Ostend and the blocking of Zeebrugge harbour. On most of those sorties the paddle minesweepers took their places at the "front of the queue" and ushered their comrades safely to and from the Belgian coast.

REMARKS.

(1)   With reference to the Paddle Mine Sweepers being attacked by hostile aircraft, I beg to submit that these vessels be supplied with a good and efficient anti-aircraft gun.

During these operations, the paddle sweepers have always been attacked and have always when attacked been in a position to attack the aircraft from an advantageous position, but having nothing but rifles are powerless.

If anti-aircraft guns are supplied not only would the Paddle sweepers be in a position to defend themselves but could with advantage take the offensive against aircraft attacking the Monitors etc.,

(2)   Sweeping ahead of a Fleet at night at slow speed.

Efficient sweeping cannot be carried out at a speed of less than 7 knots, as when going at a less speed the kites are continually coming to the surface.

It is therefore suggested that in future operations the Sweepers may be detailed to sweep certain passages and areas before the arrival of the Fleet and not endeavour to sweep just ahead of it.

If the course to be taken by the Fleet is given to the M.S.O. just before sailing, he could ensure that actual track being thoroughly swept.

I understand the object of the Sweepers is to ascertain if mines are in the vicinity and should they be found the progress of the Fleet must in all probability be delayed, but the track can be reported clear.

This can be carried out far more effectively is sweeping is carried out at a good sweeping speed. i.e. 9 to 10 knots.

The remarks submitted by Commander Walter Rigg to the Vice-A

ESCORT

    I would suggest that the escort of the Mine Sweepers should be if possible two destroyers, one of which should be near enough to the mine sweeping Officer so that immediate information can be given him and the other one following astern.

    If this were done, information could be passed to your Flag with the least possible delay and puts the destroyer in the must advantageous position for attacking hostile submarines.

    In conclusion I beg to submit that the Officers and men of the Paddle mine Sweepers having carried out their work in a very satisfactory manner.

    I would specially bring to your notice the name of Lieutenant R.J.Carruthers R.N.V.R.

    This Officer is second in Command of "MARMION 11" but during the absence of Lieutenant H.Boothby, D.S.O. R.N. on sick leave, has been in command of this vessel during the whole of the operations commencing on the 24th September.

    I cannot speak too highly of the manner in which this officer has worked his ship and his men.

          I have the honour to be,

            Sir,

              Your obedient Servant.

Vice Admiral Dover Patrol.

...er following one of the early bombing raids on the Belgian coast

PRO Ref: ADM137/2111

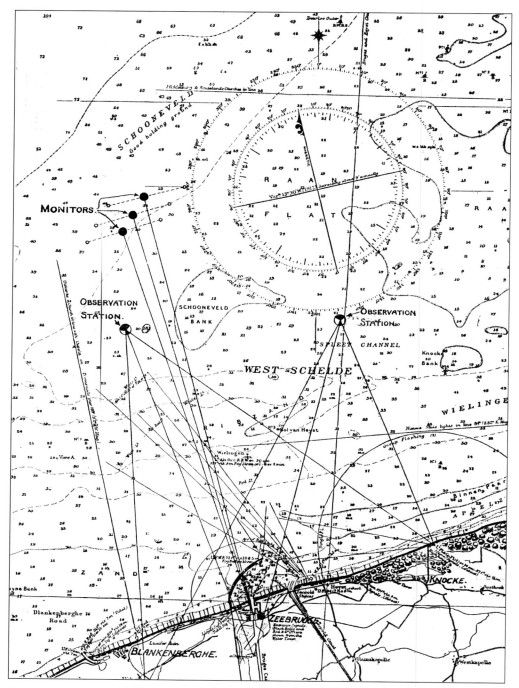

A section of a chart showing the positions of the monitors and observation stations during one of the early Belgiun coast bombardments.

PRO Ref: ADM53/33257

HMS *WESTWARD HO* in the North Sea during the autumn of 1915.

HMS *DEVONIA* explodes a mine in her
sweep in the autumn of 1915.

HMS *BRIGHTON QUEEN* in the North Sea, 1915.

HMS *LADY ISMAY* steams past a stray mine in the murky waters of the North Sea on 23rd May 1915. The crew of the armed yacht HMS *SAGITTA*, from which this photograph was taken, later sank the mine with rifle fire.

PRO Ref: ADM137/1067

For long periods throughout 1915 the Grimsby Paddlers strengthened the forces of the Dover Patrol and were based at Dunkirk. In addition to assisting in the bombarding operations they swept the sea-lanes along the barrage of mines and mine-nets laid by the Royal Navy about twelve miles off the Belgian coast between Nieuport and the Scheldt estuary. In the German reports of their actions the steamers were described as "light cruisers"; as an officer of the *DEVONIA* remarked, "Very light!" The first night-sweeping operations had been carried out in connection with the Belgian coast bombardments but by the autumn of 1915 they had become a matter of routine. They were, however, proving to be particularly alarming experiences. Lieut. Muhlhauser recounts an incident which took place while his ship, the *SAGITTA*, was sweeping with the *CAMBRIDGE*:-

"Just after 0200, off Dunkirk, a violent explosion occured between us and the Cambridge and we each thought the other had been blown up. The fact that she did not reply to our flashing signals confirmed the view that the Cambridge had gone. Our commander hailed her through a megaphone, 'Cambridge ahoy'. Her commander eventually replied. It was a great relief to hear him, though our commander's voice did not show any joy. On the contrary, anxiety as to the Cambridge's fate, added to the strain of the night's work, caused him to depart from his usual courteous manner. 'Why don't you pay attention to my signals?', he demanded - Pause - 'Why don't you answer them, damn you?' The Cambridge's commander later informed him of the reason for his inattention; he had only one signalman, who was unable to read the signal, and he himself was too busy finding out whether the ship was damaged to attend to it. On this occasion the explosion, which was caused by two mines in the sweep striking together, caused no damage."

Sir Archibald Hood, in his book, "The Merchant Navy", states:-

"Minesweeping during the hours of darkness always proved an intensely nerve-racking and perilous operation. On many occasions long distance torpedoes were fired at the paddlers while sweeping, and often, star-shells were discharged from the shore, brilliantly lighting up the ships and rendering them easily recognisable targets."

It was during one of those "perilous operations" that the first loss among the paddle steamers occured. At 01.45 on Monday 6th October 1915, the *DEVONIA, GLEN AVON, WESTWARD HO* and *BRIGHTON QUEEN* were sweeping along the Belgian coast. Four miles off Nieuport pier, in the West Deep, they were about to turn and head for Dunkirk when the *BRIGHTON QUEEN* struck a mine which exploded under her paddle box and tore her into two halves, both of which sank within minutes. Boats were immediately lowered from her three consorts and all but 7 of the crew of 41 were saved: those lost were the third engineer, three stokers and three sailors. The ships then anchored in Dunkirk Roads and later that morning four of the survivors were taken to hospital in Dunkirk, while the rest returned to Dover aboard the torpedo boat HMS *VIKING*. The sinking of the *BRIGHTON QUEEN* brought home the great danger of sweeping at night. To quote Sir Archibald Hood once more:-

> "The loss of the Brighton Queen was a matter of particular regret. This excursion steamer had been the first paddler to be taken up in 1914, and had during the following months assisted in the destruction of mines whose total value was much greater than her own. She had been the means of saving a considerable amount of shipping as well as many lives, and had been most busily employed in many parts of the North Sea, wherever, indeed, a new minefield had to be swept up. As the Admiral in charge of minesweepers remarked: 'With mines below and bombs from above, in addition to torpedoes from submarines and heavy gunfire from the shore, these sweepers have so far borne something of a charmed life which could hardly be expected to continue indefinitely.' The Brighton Queen was called upon to pay the price."

Even in daylight the sweepers ran a grave risk of striking mines which lurked, unseen, just below the surface. Such an incident occurred on Saturday 29th November 1915 when the Clyde paddle steamer, *DUCHESS OF HAMILTON*, fell victim to a mine when sweeping with the *WESTWARD HO* at the northern end of the Black Deep, 19 miles SE of Harwich, with the loss of nine of her crew.

A similar tragedy followed three weeks later when the White Funnel steamer, *LADY ISMAY,* was lost near the Longsand Lightvessel, in the Thames estuary. The following account is based on the report of the Flotilla Commander, Lieut. William V. Rice of the *DEVONIA*, which was submitted at the official Admiralty Inquiry.

On the morning of Tuesday 21st December 1915 the paddle minesweepers *YARMOUTH BELLE, DEVONIA, QUEEN EMPRESS, WESTWARD HO, CAMBRIDGE, GLEN AVON* and *LADY ISMAY* left Harwich to sweep an area to the south-east. At about noon, visibility deteriorated; the former three vessels became separated from the others and proceeded towards Harwich. A wireless message was sent to the other group informing them of that fact but it was not received.

At 15.00 Lieut. Buckland, in the *WESTWARD HO*, gave the order to slip sweeps, and then set a course for the Longsand Lightvessel. The ships were in single line ahead with the *WESTWARD HO* leading, followed by the *CAMBRIDGE, LADY ISMAY* and *GLEN AVON*. At 15.30 the *WESTWARD HO* passed the Longsand Lightvessel two cables on the starboard hand; the *CAMBRIDGE* also passed the lightvessel on the starboard hand. The *LADY ISMAY,* about three-quarters of a mile astern, passed the lightvessel on the port hand, being set to the northward by the tide. The *WESTWARD HO* then set a course from the lightvessel, N30W, speed 12 knots. At about 15.40 the *LADY ISMAY* struck a mine which exploded underneath the forward bunkers, amidships, and sank within one minute.

Her Second Engineer, John Taylor, a son of the Commodore of the White Funnel Fleet, Capt. Dan Taylor, was on deck at the time of the explosion and later stated:-

"I would never have imagined that a ship could sink so quickly; not a man on deck so much as got his feet wet, they simply stepped into the lifeboats as she went down."

The *GLEN AVON,* having been slightly astern of the *LADY ISMAY,* was on the scene first; her boats were lowered and she began to pick up the survivors. The *CAMBRIDGE* and *WESTWARD HO* immediately turned back, the former also lowered boats, picked up survivors and destroyed all the *LADY ISMAY'S* confidential papers, which were floating on the surface of the water.

Lieut. Ralph Cooke, commander of the *CAMBRIDGE,* reported that he had passed a Swedish steamer about one mile on his port beam, steering a parallel course in the opposite direction, about five minutes before the explosion: he had not seen her name. Other reports were received concerning this vessel which at one time was seen drifting, with what appeared to be a derrick of some sort projecting from her stern. Whether or not this vessel was, in fact, German and had been laying mines, one of which was responsible for the loss of the *LADY ISMAY,* was never established. By the time the rescue had taken place the vessel had disappeared.

The Board of Inquiry submitted its report to the Admiralty and confirmed that, after careful examination of several witnesses, it was of the opinion that the *LADY ISMAY* had been sunk by a mine and not by a torpedo, which at one time had been suspected. The report also brought to the attention of the Admiralty the gallant action of two officers:-

"After the wreck of the Lady Ismay the Glen Avon approached to assist in saving the men in the water. Lieut. J. Collis Bird, commander of the Glen Avon, seeing two men in great danger of drowning, dived off the forecastle of his ship, without taking off any of his clothing, and kept them afloat until rescued by boat. But for this prompt action, the men would undoubtedly have perished.

William Carter, Mate of the Lady Ismay, was thrown into the water by the explosion but managed to climb on to a life-raft. When Petty Officer Bell, who was badly injured, came to the surface, Carter, with great difficulty, hauled him on to the raft. Bell was now unconscious and, although himself exhausted, Carter proceeded to attempt to revive him by artificial respiration. When the boat from the Cambridge came to pick them up, Carter sent it away to pick up the men who were still in the water and continued with his attempts to revive Bell, but in spite of every exertion the unfortunate man expired. Carter was then the last man to be picked up."

In the last few months of 1915 three paddle minesweepers had been lost as a consequence of striking mines: each had sunk within minutes and their losses had claimed nearly forty lives. Despite the many precautionary procedures which were followed, there was no sure way of avoiding such catastrophes.

It is difficult to convey any adequate impression of the dangers which the crews of the minesweepers faced during the course of their duties. On one occasion, as the survivors of a mine explosion clung to liferafts in the water, they could only watch as several of their comrades, trapped on the lower deck of their rapidly sinking ship, cried for help through the open portholes. Their exit had been blocked by damage from the explosion and the portholes were barely big enough for their heads to pass through. Both they and their more fortunate comrades knew that there was no escape, and that death was inevitable. Such incidents, which shocked and horrified even the most resilient of spirits, only made the survivors more determined to get back to the job and defeat the German mine menace, despite the perils which they knew were ever present.

The former Royal Naval officer, Capt. Taprell Dorling, in his book, "Swept Channels", perfectly epitomised their situation:-

> "The unostentatious heroism of those who continued to work in the minesweepers, after once being blown up or having seen their friends blown up, can hardly be exaggerated. They had none of the excitement of battle against a visible foe - nothing of the supreme satisfaction of being able to hit back. The work was entirely one sided - 'Heads you win. Tails I lose'."

The "unostentatious heroism" referred to by Capt. Dorling was exemplified by Frank Louis Niblett, Chief Petty Officer of the *BRIGHTON QUEEN*.

In conversation with his grandson, Mr John Niblett, the author was told the story, passed down through the family, of how Frank Niblett, in his mid-30's, enlisted in the Gloucestershire Regiment in the early months of the war. On the following day he learned that the Campbell steamers were being requisitioned. As an experienced skipper of one of the tugs owned by the King family of Bristol, he naturally felt that his capabilities would be put to better use in the Royal Navy. He enlisted forthwith and sailed from Bristol almost immediately, it is believed in the *LADY ISMAY*.

He was Chief Petty Officer in the *BRIGHTON QUEEN* at the time of her sinking. After he had been rescued and returned to Dover he volunteered for further minesweeping duties and was again a survivor when his second ship was mined.

His determined and undaunted spirit led him to join a third minesweeper in which he again survived a mine explosion. On this occasion he was invalided out of the Navy and returned to his tug duties.

On his death in 1943 his obituaries paid tribute to his outstanding service record and were justly lavish in their praise of the tug skipper who went to war.

Unostentatious heroism indeed!

23

H.M.S. " Glen - Avon " " Wednesday day of 6th Octr, 1915.
From Sweeping Ground, To Dunkerque and Dunkerque.

Hours	Patent Log — Distance Run		Standard Compass Courses	Deviation of Standard Compass	Revolutions per minute	Wind		Weather	State of the Sea	Height of Barometer and Attached Thermo-meter	Temperature			Position			REMARKS	Initials of the Officer of the Watch
	Miles	Tenths				Direction	Force				Air	Wet Bulb	Sea	8.0 a.m. — Latitude / Longitude				
																	A.M.	
1	1	0	Name of Men Lost from the			NE.	2	c	S					1·45 a.m. Slipped the buoys & proceeded towards Pt. Queen, which was shewn up by a mine & foundered.	
2	6	0	Brighton Queen = on board Glen Avon	J. Stubby Mate										1·50 transmd all boats and went to her assistance	
3	6	0	G. Lidell 2nd Eng	G. Lemmon 2nd Hand										7 men brought on board Glen Avon by Brighton boat.	
4	6	0	J.W. Geelin Seaman	J.W. Hendrie Cook					30·30						
5			E.E. Clark Seaman	W. Senior Seaman											
6			5·an am this day the H.M.S. Viking came alongside to											2·30 proceeded towards Dunkerque Ra. 3·15 arrived outside Dunkerque.	
7			tele off Brighton Queen causing damage	Seamen same work and Code Light siren										3/20 dropped Star & 7 fthm. 2 shackles hands pipe down	
8						Calm blue smooth sea				29·72					at ↓ stiff Dunkerque Ra.	
9			2 Wanderers sent on leave with											9·00 weighed & proceeded into Harbour	
10	7	0	Brighton Queen Survivors & not returned											9·15 moored alongside Quaywall 11·00 cast off and proceeded to Coal Wharf	
11	4	0												12·30 moored to S.S. Luxembourg for Coal	

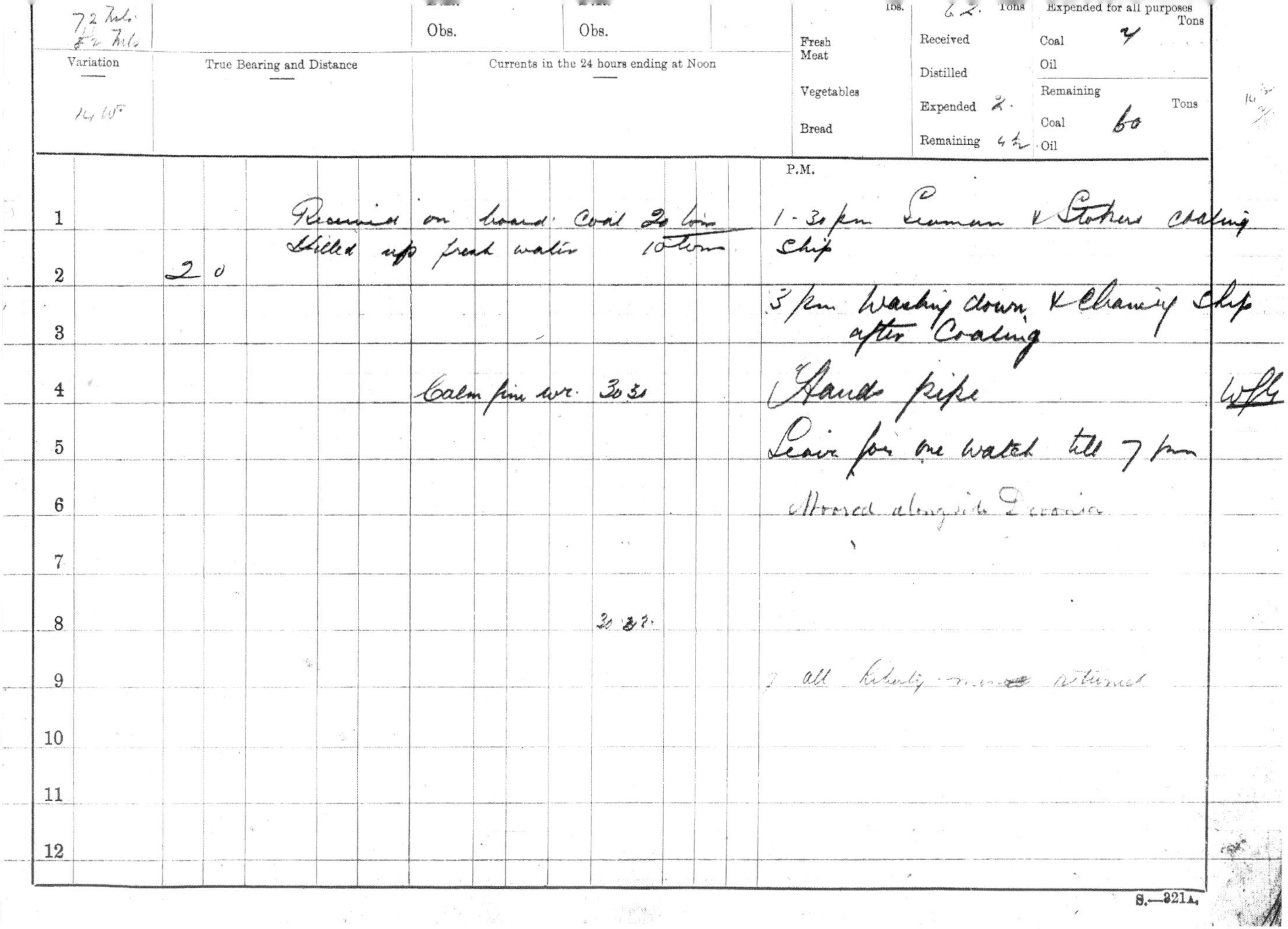

			Fresh Meat		Received		Tons	Expended for all purposes Tons
					Coal	Oil		Coal 4
			Vegetables		Distilled			Oil
					Expended 2			Remaining
			Bread		Remaining 4 4 Oil		Tons	Coal 60

(Handwritten ship's log table, P.M. entries, hours 1–12)

- 1. Remained on board. April 24 live ... 10 tons ... 1-3 pm Seamen & Stokers cooking ship
- 2. Filled up feed water ... 20 ...
- 3. 3 pm Washing down & cleaning ship after coaling
- 4. Calm fine ... ave. 3.3 ... Speke pipe ... 4/4
- 5. Oar for the watch till 7 pm
- 6.
- 7.
- 8. 2.37
- 9. Arrived alongside ... Attend ... cordite ...
- 10.
- 11.
- 12.

Variation: 14 10 ... 2 0

S.—221a.

The log of HMS *GLEN AVON* for Wednesday 6th October 1915; detailing her actions during and after the loss of the *BRIGHTON QUEEN*.
PRO Ref: ADM53/42885

Dear Sir

Just a line asking you information about the *Lady Ismay* as I am sorry to say it has been reported missing and I should like to hear the full particulars and would feel more settled if we could hear the right news as

is my main support We recieved the news that the boat and the crew were all missing and I should like to know for the sake of the two children hoping to hear from you at the earliest moment

I remain

Miss

A letter from a lady to the Admiralty enquiring as to the fate of her partner - one of the personnel of the *LADY ISMAY*.

PRO Ref: ADM1/8442/361

IMMEDIATE

Dear Sir just a line asking you information of the ship Lady Ismay I received the news of it being blown up and I would be pleased if you would give me information I have been speaking to some of the crews wifes and you have sent them the news and I have wrote before but received

no answer from you yet. I should be more settled if you let me have the information of for the sake of my children hoping to hear from you soon I have inquired at the Peakin office and they told me he was amongst the missing and said it would be wise for me to write you which I did last week and

am still waiting for a reply. I really cannot think it it true that he has been taken away from us so sudden but I must trust in the Lord to take care of the two children

I remain

Miss

Having received no reply, a second letter was sent a week later. The couple were not married, and it appears that the social stigma attached to such relationships in those days meant that the Admiralty had no record of the lady as next of kin. The "Peakin office" referred to in the letter was, in fact, HMS Pekin, the shore base at Grimsby from which Capt. Massey-Dawson controlled the operations of the north-east coast minesweeping flotillas.
PRO Ref: ADM1/8442/361

January 1916.

Madam,

In reply to your letters received on the 29th.
December and 5th January, I regret to have to inform you that
H.M.S. "LADY ISMAY" was blown up by a mine on the 21st.
December and that

lost his life on that occasion.

Any application which the next of kin or legal
representative of the deceased may have to make in consequence
of the foregoing information should be made by letter addressed
to the Accountant General of the Navy, Admiralty, London, S.W.

I am, Madam,

Your obedient Servant,

Accountant General
of the Navy.

The situation was, however, soon resolved by the Admiralty's somewhat terse reply. (The names of the parties
have been removed to preserve confidentiality).

PRO Ref: ADM1/8442/361

R.N. Hospital,

S H O T L E Y.

25th December 1915.

Sir,

     With reference to the loss of the P.M.S. "Lady Ismay"
I have the honour to make the following report :-

     On Tuesday 21 Dec. 1915 having completed sweeping
operations in the P.M.S. "Lady Ismay" under my command, I was
returning to Harwich, when at about 3 .37 p.m. Longsand Light
Vessel S 40 E 5 cables approx' the "Lady Ismay" struck a
mine amidships, she foundered in half a minute, there being
no time to man boats or take other measures for the saving of
life. We were thrown violently into the water and I fear
only those actually on deck survived.

     Before the disaster the P.M.S's, were in single line
ahead", Cambridge"being ahead of me and "Glen Avon" astern.

     These two vessels rendered every possible assistance in
picking up survivors. Great credit is due to their Commanding
Officers Lieut. Collin Bird R.N., and Lieut. Cook R.N.R., for
the rapidity with which they carried out this duty, and many of
us feel that we owe our lives to their prompt action and
seamanship.

               I have the honour, to be,

                    Sir,

               Your obedient Servant,

               B. W. Hawken, Sub. Lieut. R.N.R.

omanding Officer,

P.M.S.O. Grimsby.

               Lately in Command,
                  H.M. P.M.S. "Lady Ismay"

The report of the loss of HMS *LADY ISMAY* sent by her commander from the Royal Naval Hospital at Shotley, Harwich, on Christmas Day 1915. The head injuries sustained by Sub-Lieut. Hawken from the explosion were responsible for the delay in the issuing of his report. He made a full recovery, however, and in the years following the war became one of P. & A. Campbell's most respected masters.

PRO Ref: ADM137/3128

P. & A. CAMPBELL, LIMITED.

DIRECTORS' REPORT.

To be submitted at the Twenty Fourth Ordinary General Meeting to be held at the Grand Hotel, Bristol, on Tuesday, May 9th, 1916, at 12 noon.

The Directors beg to present herewith a Summary of the Balance Sheet made up to the 31st day of December last, by which it will be seen that after payment of Interest on the Preference Shares at the rate of Six per cent. per annum and an Interim Dividend of Five per cent. (being at the rate of Ten per cent. per annum) on the Ordinary Shares, there remains a balance of £33,304 6s. 9d. which the Directors propose to deal with as follows :—

	£	s.	d.
To Sinking Fund (raising same to £135,000)	25,000	0	0
„ Final Dividend of Five per cent. on Ordinary Shares (free of Income Tax) making Ten per cent. for the year	2,500	0	0
„ Balance to carry forward	5,804	6	9
	£33,304	6	9

Of the Eleven Steamers requisitioned by H.M. Admiralty, two have been lost, viz. : "Brighton Queen" and "Lady Ismay," and claims for compensation have been put forward.

The Directors hope that the Steamers "Waverley" and "Glen Rosa" will re-open the Service between Cardiff and Weston at Whitsuntide.

The Directors regret to announce the death of their colleague, Mr. Edmund Handcock, in March last. They do not at present recommend that the consequent vacancy shall be filled.

Messrs. H. W. K. Wait and John Cory retire by rotation, and being eligible, offer themselves for re-election.

Messrs. Ham, Dennehy & Co., the Auditors, also retire, and offer themselves for re-election.

IVIE M. DUNLOP,
JOHN CORY, } *Directors.*

B. W. CHURCHYARD, *Secretary.*
April 29th, 1916.

ALEXANDER CAMPBELL,
Managing Director.

The P. & A. Campbell Directors Report of 1916.

HORSES FOR COURSES

"Minesweeping was not all 'Beer and Skittles'; in fact precious little 'beer', and the ships employed looked very much like 'skittles' when they came into contact with a minefield."

Capt. C. C. Bell,
Commander of a "Racecourse" paddle-minesweeper.

In May 1915 the First Lord of the Admiralty, Winston Churchill, revised his original estimate of the duration of the war. He wrote to the Admiralty departments:-

"It is to be assumed that the war will not end before 31 December 1916. All Admiralty arrangements and plans should be prepared on this basis, and any measures for the strengthening of our naval power which will become effective before that date may be considered. This applies to all questions of personnel, ships, armaments and stores, and to the organisation and maintenance of the fleet and dockyards, which must be adapted to a long period of continuing, developing strength without undue strain."

Among the "measures for the strengthening of our naval power" already in hand were plans for the building of a fleet of ships, principally for minesweeping, but also for use on a variety of general duties. The first twelve of those vessels, single screw sloops of the "Flower" class, were ordered on January 1st 1915. The ships were built remarkably quickly, delivery of the first dozen being effected between May and August 1915.

Minesweeping was gradually falling into divisions which ensured that the best type of vessels were used for each aspect of the job. The three main categories were:-

1. The Fast Sweepers, comprising the original gunboats, and minesweepers built during the war. They swept ahead of fleets and, later, convoys, and searched the approaches to fleet bases and convoy assembly ports.

2. The Routine Sweepers, consisting of trawlers and drifters, assisted by motor launches, which carried out the daily search of the war channels and approaches to harbours.

3. The Clearance Sweepers, consisting of the shallow draught paddle steamers, which cleared the minefields when located.

The paddle steamers were proving to be ideal minesweepers. They could sweep at a speed of ten to twelve knots and thus cut the moorings of the mines encountered instead of dragging them in the sweep as did the slower trawlers. Being relatively fast and powerful ships they were able to perform more work than trawlers except in really heavy weather when the fishing vessels were better able to withstand the severe conditions. However, the paddlers achievements soon dispelled any idea of their being only "fine weather ships".

Furthermore, they stood up well to the heavy duties imposed on them. Apart from the extremes of weather, they had to withstand the stresses and strains of extra weight from the cumbersome sweeping gear, twice their normal coal bunker capacity, guns, ammunition and strengthenings, as well as the concussions from the exploding of swept mines.

By May 1915, Admiral Charlton was becoming increasingly concerned about the vulnerability of the trawler minesweepers and submitted the following minute to the Admiralty:-

"On other papers I have reported the loss of yet another trawler, the Recolo, which was blown up on the 26th April 1915 near the southern limit of the Swarte Bank. A group of trawler sweepers has now been ordered to sweep the area. The paddle minesweepers were on their way to perform this duty on the 24th April when they were deflected for urgent service on the Belgian coast.

On their return they were at once sent to the Swarte Bank, where they are invaluable owing to their speed and light draught, which allows sweeping over a known minefield to continue throughout daylight hours, with little danger of their being blown up.

Trawlers are generally unable to sweep for longer than five hours each tide, ie. 2½ hours either side of high water, owing to their great draught. When fitted with bow gear their sweeping speed is barely 5 knots.

Experience has completely shown the value of paddle minesweepers of fair speed and light draught. The effect of these attributes was seen last month when they completed a sweep of 495 miles in four days on the Dogger Bank area. The same work performed by trawlers in the same time would have necessitated the use of nearly four times as many vessels, or would have taken the same number of trawlers a fortnight to carry out, even supposing that fair weather had continued for so long.

Even when there is only one minefield to be worked on at the time, the present number of paddle minesweepers on the east coast is barely sufficient. It is found that one is always under repair, which reduces the force by one third, since these vessels always work in pairs....

The enemy now seems to have awakened from his prolonged torpor in the North Sea, and it is probable that this department will again be required to dislocate the routine work proceeding on the War Channel, where the whole coastwise trade depends on the minesweepers thoroughly carrying out a dull and thankless task. Unfortunately, paddle vessels of sufficient speed and strength are not to be found.

If it should be decided that such vessels should be provided, they must be built. The cost would not be great, compared with the new minesweeping sloops, and their value would be immeasurable. Looking ahead some months, when the long nights will again facilitate it, we must expect a recrudescence of minelaying on our coasts. These fields can soon be cleared, provided sufficient light draught vessels are available.

The new single screw steamers building are valuable for minesweeping in the open sea, but their cost is comparatively great; they carry more than twice as many men as each paddle minesweeper, and draw over three feet more water.

Briefly, the requirements for the proposed Government paddle sweepers would be:-

> Sea speed of 15 knots, giving a sweeping speed of 12 knots.
> Coal and water stowage to enable them to keep at sea for a week.
> Strengthened bows and watertight sub-division.
> Light draught, not exceeding 7 feet.
> Small crew.
> Wireless telegraphy.

The paddlers are needed for war purposes; after the war, when the trawlers are released to resume their fishing, they will be required to clear the seas of the thousands of mines which may be expected to remain."

The Admiralty shared Admiral Charlton's concern regarding the vulnerability of the trawlers and agreed with his proposals. In order to obtain further guidance on the design and construction of the vessels, he was instructed to call for reports from the commanders of the six Campbell paddlers of the Grimsby flotilla. The task was entrusted to Capt. Massey-Dawson who collated the information and replied to Admiral Charlton several weeks later:-

> "..Reports as called for herewith. No particular vessel embodies all the desired features. A draft specification for the most suitable type of vessel, by Lt. Sanders, is submitted. This officer has had considerable experience with vessels of this type."

Lieut. Arthur L. Sanders, it will be remembered, was the main instigator behind the use of paddle steamers as minesweepers in the first instance. In his report, headed "HMS Brighton Queen, Grimsby", he began by stating, "This ship is the most suitable of those in the Grimsby Paddler Section", and then continued in great detail of a technical nature regarding the hull construction and machinery of the proposed new vessels. Among a variety of modifications he advocated the use of a pair of gallows on either side of the deck, just aft of the paddle boxes, with a powerful winch between them; an arrangement which would allow the ships to work in groups of three or more, thus extending the sweeping area.

Lieut. Sanders' suggestions were the most radical, but in general, the commanders agreed on the main drawbacks of the steamers as they stood and called for larger anchor gear, more powerful winches and greater coal and water capacity.

The recommendations were, in the main, accepted by the Admiralty, although the twin gallows feature was not implemented. One innovation which must have been particularly welcome, however, was the addition of wheelhouses.

The Campbell minesweepers still retained their open bridges with no more

SECRET.

Copy.

The question of building additional shallow draught
paddle steamers for use as mine sweepers is under
consideration, and to expedite progress and ensure providing
what is most suitable, it is desired to have information
so far as may be quickly and conveniently available, as on
table herewith for each vessel named below.

It is also desired that an opinion should be given as
to whether any particular vessels embody at present all the
principal features desired and so may be taken xxxxx as a
standard type for the new ships. If there are any features
in the respective vessels which are distinctly undesirable,
to be reproduced in the new vessels, they should be stated
against the names of the vessels.

Name.	Features to be recommended for new design.	Features to be avoided in new design.
"Brighton Queen".		
"Devonia".		
"Cambridge".		
"Westward Ho".		
"Glen Avon".		
"Lady Ismay".		

(handwritten, bracketing the vessel names: Stronger & larger windlanes Yes / Evaporation to be fitted / Reserve feed winds tanks for boilers) *(handwritten, second bracket: Hay stack boilers — Yes)*

Information desired for each ship.

List of Anchors.

Cables.

Boats.

Complement.

Armament.

Height of Masts.

Material of Masts (wood or iron).

Type of W/T fitted. *(handwritten: none fitted)*

(handwritten bracket spanning Cables through Height of Masts: as per lists enclosed)

The letter sent by Capt. Massey-Dawson to each of the commanders of the Grimsby paddlers, in

86

If fitted with   *see lists enclosed*

    Steam windlass *yes*

    "   steering gear *yes*

    "   winch (in addition to trawl winch).

    Evaporators and Distillers, and capacity of same.

Approximate weight when fully loaded.

    Provisions.   Mine Sweeping stores & outfit.

    Officers Stores.   Ammunition.

    Paymasters Stores.   Coal (Bunkers full).

    Canteen Stores.   Water:- Drinking

    W.O's Stores.   Reserve Feed.

    Engineers Stores.   In Feed Tanks.

Draught. Fully loaded on leaving harbour. Forward. Aft.

    Light; coal and stores used out.   "   ".

Speed. (a) Maximum for short spurt.

    (b) For a period of 6 or 8 hours.

    (c) When sweeping.

Approximate diameter of turning circle.

Is manoeuvring power satisfactory ?

29 MAY 1915

tain guidance on the design and construction of the proposed Admiralty paddle minesweepers.

PRO Ref: ADM1/8420/123

protection against the weather than a canvas dodger. However, the advent of additional shelter being provided on the Government paddlers led to similar "extensions" being constructed on the excursion vessels. They were made of teak and were fitted during the winter of 1915/1916. There were exceptions, however: they were the *ALBYN*, which did not receive a wheelhouse but instead was fitted with deck shelters at the extremities of both port and starboard bridge wings, and the *BRIGHTON QUEEN* and *LADY ISMAY*, which had been lost before they received the benefit of this luxury.

The question of which shipbuilder should be entrusted to produce the final plans for the Admiralty paddlers was next considered.

The Ailsa Shipbuilding Co. of Troon had built P. & A. Campbell's last three new ships; the *LADY ISMAY* in 1911, the *GLEN AVON* in 1912 and their "masterpiece", the *GLEN USK*, in 1914. Of this outstanding trio of ships the design of the *GLEN USK* was considered to be the best suited to embody the requirements and accordingly, although the Admiralty vessels were to be over ten feet longer than the prototype, their hulls were designed on virtually the same lines.

The Ailsa Shipbuilding Co's minute books contain the following entries:-

> "26 August 1915. A verbal order has recently been received from the Admiralty for two new paddle minesweepers, the contract price for which would be arranged later. There is a possibility of securing the order of a third, similar vessel if satisfactory delivery could be guaranteed. Material is being ordered for two vessels..."

> "Telegram received from the Admiralty on 28th August 1915 stating that they are prepared to authorise the company to proceed with work on the two paddle steamers in accordance with the design prepared by Ailsa, on the following conditions; viz. that the company will submit a firm price and state the shortest time for delivery, and agree to leave to the Admiralty the final decision as to the amounts to be paid.
> The telegram further requested the Ailsa company to name prices for the preparation of general drawings and calculations, working ship drawings and machinery drawings for the guidance of other firms; the number of firms not to exceed ten.
> Reported that a reply had been sent to the Admiralty accepting their offer on the conditions named in their telegram, and that the prices for the vessels and for preparing drawings will be submitted to the Admiralty shortly..."

> "Telegram received from the Admiralty on 1st October 1915 accepting the company's tender, dated 22nd September, for a third paddle steamer to be constructed at Troon, for delivery in eight months. Reported that the Admiralty had not yet intimated their decision regarding the price of the two similar vessels ordered on 23rd August."

The engines of the Admiralty paddlers were to be identical to those of the *GLEN USK*, but one aspect of their machinery was to be different, and this was to be one of their drawbacks.

The *GLEN USK* had been fitted with a single boiler, but the Admiralty did not leave well enough alone; their specification stated:-

> "Machinery installation will be the same as that of the Glen Usk except that two boilers of equal power will be provided instead of one large boiler. Machinery will be disposed in three separate compartments instead of two."

The principal behind the installation of twin boilers was sound in that they were to be used alternately - the boiler not in use being blown down for cleaning and maintenance at sea, thus reducing the time spent out of action for such purposes. However, equal power does not mean equal weight, and the extra burden of the additional boiler meant that the same efficient running, consistently maintained by the *GLEN USK*, was not to be forthcoming with the Admiralty vessels. During the course of their deliberations, the Admiralty frequently consulted Capt. Peter Campbell on a variety of technical matters, whose advice was, in the main, put into practice. Capt. Peter clearly stated that the proposed twin boilers would increase the ships' displacement tonnage by approximately 250 over that of the *GLEN USK*, and that consequently the ships would be underpowered. Nevertheless, on the boiler question, Capt. Peter was overruled and the Admiralty proceeded with their original plans.

Each ship was to carry two 12-pounder guns and one 3" anti-aircraft gun. They were to have two masts, derricks and stowage for a seaplane, so that an anti-Zeppelin patrol could be maintained some distance off the coast. Owing to the urgent need for minesweepers, however, the seaplane idea was abandoned. They were to have a complement of 7 officers and 43 men, and each vessel cost about £55,000.

The result was a class of vessels named after UK racecourses, of which 32 were ordered from a variety of shipyards between August 1915 and January 1917. The first 24 appeared in 1916, and by the end of the year nearly all were in service in the principal danger areas, being stationed at Dover, Lowestoft, Grimsby and on the Firth of Forth. They were followed in 1918 by the eight vessels of the "Improved" Racecourse class, which were four feet longer and with a slightly increased gross tonnage.

In appearance the vessels of the Racecourse class bore little resemblance to the *GLEN USK*, the main difference being the former's two widely spaced funnels as opposed to the *GLEN USK'S* one. However, their dimensions were similar and their lines and hull construction were virtually identical.

By the end of 1915 the sweeping force of hired paddle steamers had grown to five units, comprising thirty-five vessels. They were supplemented by the first of the Racecourse class in April 1916.

Capt. C. C. Bell DSO. RN. took command of a unit of six of them, the *TOTNES* unit, and expressed his opinion of their performance:-

> "They were...somewhat akin to the mercantile paddlers that are so well known on the south coast and in the Bristol Channel. My Chief Engineer, Augustus Slocombe, was a Royal Naval Reservist, sub-lieutenant engineer - a pre-war chief engineer of one of Campbell's Bristol Channel paddlers, and an excellent man at his job.
> Unfortunately the Glen Usk had been taken as a pattern, whereas if they

had been modelled on the Devonia a much better sweeper would have evolved. The latter vessel is the finest paddle sweeper I have ever met; she could sweep rings round any Admiralty paddler.

...they were good sea-boats, though most uncomfortable in a beam sea, or in fact any sea when there was a roll on. You never finished the roll - crash went the sponson to check the roll when it was half through, squirting fountains of water over the whole ship.

In a strong head sea, sweeping was impossible, as the ships would not steer with a sweep wire towing astern. The paddle wheels were on the same shaft and could not be disconnected to work independently, and as there was no splash to the rudder, as in screw vessels, the result was that the ships became, in minesweeping language, "Doggo", ie. they lay helpless, stern to stern. There was nothing left to do then but slip sweeps and start again..."

Capt. Bell also commented on their lack of power, which he attributed to their paddle wheels being too small. In fact, the diameter of their wheels was identical to that of the *GLEN USK*, which had already proved to be ideally suited to the engines. Once again, the fault lay in the extra weight of the additional boiler.

Furthermore, instead of the fan shaped vents of the *GLEN USK*, the paddle-box facings were given narrow, concentric slat openings, thus providing insufficient ventilation, consequently the paddles frequently became choked with water, exacerbating their, often, sluggish progress. This particular problem was highlighted when the ships became the subject of an Admiralty Confidential Order of 4th May 1917 which stated:-

"Racecourse class more seaworthy and better sweeping speed when bunkers only half full. Arrangements to be made for vessels to bunker accordingly with 75/80 tons of coal. It appears that the liability of the paddle boxes to choke would be reduced with vessels in this condition."

Thus, the Admiralty's requirement for increased coal capacity was to remain unfulfilled.

Nevertheless, in spite of their shortcomings the vessels performed well and, without doubt, helped to ease the burden which fell so heavily on the minesweeping service.

In conclusion, a further quote from Capt. Bell is appropriate, relating to the time when he was in command of HMS *TOTNES*. The ship was returning alone to Lowestoft, and a full SE gale was blowing straight into the harbour entrance:-

"...To my amazement I received the order to enter harbour...I thought it was sheer lunacy, but I'd sooner be in than out. So I proceeded to make the most thrilling entry into harbour I've ever made.

There was a very heavy following sea, and a strong tide across the entrance. A sea right astern is the worst possible for handling paddlers, as you have no wash from the propellers to help steering, and the rudder at times is right out of the water. However, it was a case of do or die, so putting the telegraph to full speed I made for the entrance, the ship yawing horribly from side to side, heading first for one pier and then the other. I well remember my officer of the watch gasping, 'You'll never do it, sir!' The next moment we charged crab-fashion through the entrance to be hailed by the pilot, 'Stop, for God's sake, stop! I'm coming on board!' As I put the engines to full astern I shouted, 'Too late, George, you can't help now!' and just managed to bring her up short of the road bridge across the harbour without a scratch. Personally I thought the chances ten to one against our getting in unscathed; but I resolved never again to come in in a south-easterly gale whatever my orders!"

GLEN USK (Ailsa Yard No. 287)		**ASCOT** (Ailsa Yard No. 297)	
Length (OA)	231ft. 3ins.	245ft. 9ins.	
Length (BP)	224ft. 6ins.	235ft. 0ins.	
Breadth (moulded)	28ft. 0ins.	29ft. 0ins.	
Extreme breadth	56ft. 0ins.	57ft. 0ins.	
Depth (moulded)	9ft. 0ins.	9ft. 6ins.	
Draught	6ft. 8ins.	6ft. 9ins.	
Horsepower (IHP)	1578	1566	
Speed (knots)	17.17	15.02	
	(Best on trials, 27/5/14)	(Best on trials, 11/4/16)	
Engines	Compound 2-cyl	Compound 2-cyl	
Cylinders, ins.	HP-26½, LP-52	HP-26½, LP-52	
Stroke.	54ins.	54ins.	
Tonnage, net	225.63	304.86	
No. of decks	2	2	
Bulkheads	5	11	
Sheer, foward	36ins.	30ins.	
Sheer, aft	13ins.	7½ins.	
Boilers	1	2	
	(16ft. x 11ft. 6ins.)	(13ft. 3ins. x 10ft. 9ins.)	
Boiler pressure	125lbs.	125lbs.	
Paddles	7 float wheel	7 float wheel	
Floats	(10ft. 3ins. x 2ft. 11½ins.)	(11ft. x 3ft.)	

Comparative dimensions of HMS *GLEN USK* and the first of the Admiralty paddle minesweepers, HMS *ASCOT*, compiled from the records of the Ailsa Shipbuilding Co. Ltd. of Troon.

The second of the Racecourse class paddle minesweepers, HMS *ERIDGE*, built by the Clyde Shipbuilding Co. and delivered in April 1916.

IWM Ref: Q43247

HMS *PONTEFRACT.*

IWM Ref: SP2991

HMS *ATHERSTONE*, built by the Ailsa Shipbuilding Co. and delivered in June 1916. This vessel was later to become the new Medway Steam Packet Company's *QUEEN OF KENT*.

IWM Ref: SP106

HMS *KEMPTON*, one of the Racecourse class war losses. She sank after striking a mine off the French coast on 24th June 1917.

IWM Ref: SP1649

An unidentified paddler of the Racecourse class.

IWM Ref: Q43375

An unidentified paddler of the Racecourse class, with additional deckhouses on the after deck.

IWM Ref: SP2403

HMS *EPSOM.*

95

Towards the end of the war, in the course of their mine clearance duties, several members of the Racecourse class travelled far beyond home waters. In this unique photograph HMS *HALDON* lies outside HMS *LADAS*, the flagship of the Rear Admiral, White Sea, at Archangel in the USSR.

BROIL AND BATTLE

"I am afraid I cannot do justice to all I feel about the work of these men. Necessarily, it is little known to the public. They do not work in the presence of great bodies of men to applaud and admire them for their gallantry. Small crews in stormy seas suddenly face to face with unexpected peril, they never seem to fail. No danger, no difficulty is too great for them. The debt of this country to them is incalculable."

Arthur Balfour, First Lord of the Admiralty; speaking in the House of Commons of the personnel of the minesweeping forces. 7th March 1916

Scotland.

As soon as the first of the war-built, "Flower" class minesweeping sloops had been completed, in mid-1915, they joined the units of the Grand Fleet based on Scotland's north-east coast. At the end of the year they replaced the paddle sweepers in the Moray Firth. Admiral Jellicoe wrote to Lieut. Commander Heaton on 18th December 1915:-

"Experience has shown that the paddlers are unfit for sweeping in the open sea, in the north during the winter months, and that their anchor gear is unsuitable for any but well sheltered anchorages. Under these circumstances it is suggested that they should be based at Leith and employed sweeping inside May Island.

The *GLEN USK* led the flotilla southward to the Firth of Forth in January 1916. Their orders were slightly amended, however, and they were based, not at Leith, but a short distance away at Granton. From there they swept a large area from Inchkeith Island to the Isle of May, and during the summer months, northward towards Bell Rock and southward towards Bass Rock. Their main duties were to protect the entrances and exits of the ships of the Grand Fleet and later, the clearing of channels for the departures of the east coast and Scandinavian convoys from their assembly points off Methil, in Largo Bay.

The flotilla remained in the Firth of Forth for the duration of the war and met with little incident, apart from one occasion when the *BRITAIN* experienced a very narrow escape. After thoroughly sweeping a stretch of water, a new mine, just awash and hardly visible was seen dead ahead in line with her bow, about 25 yards away. Fortunately the keen-eyed lookout in the bow had spotted it and immediately shouted and signalled to the bridge. Avoiding action was taken just in time and the *BRITAIN* steamed past the mine with only inches to spare. Having reached a safe distance, the ship was stopped and the crew destroyed the mine with rifle fire and, no doubt, a great deal of relish!

HMS *GLEN USK*, complete with wheelhouse.

HMS *GLEN USK* approaches the stern of a Racecourse paddler to join sweeps in the Firth of Forth .

HMS *BRITAIN*.

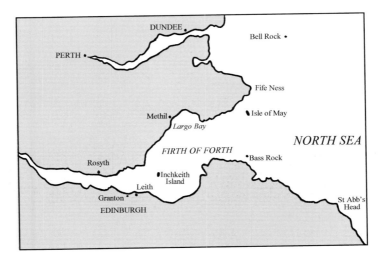

The Firth of Forth.

Zeppelins.

In February 1916 Admiral von Pohl, who had replaced von Ingenohl early in 1915, died, and was succeeded, as Commander in Chief of the High Seas Fleet, by Vice-Admiral Reinhard Scheer, a man determined to follow more aggressive policies, one of which was a wider use of the Zeppelins.

During the Great War Germany produced 88 of these gas-filled, lighter-than-air ships and used them mainly for reconnaissance purposes, particularly as protection against naval attacks. However, since early 1915, they had been sent on a number of bombing raids on British cities and to counter the threat to civilians, a blackout was imposed, with searchlights and anti-aircraft batteries being installed in key areas.

On the night of 31st March 1916 Zeppelin L15 was flying over London, one of a number which had been sent out earlier that day, their objective being to bomb the munitions factories in and around London. At 22.45 searchlights at Dartford picked her up and the ensuing anti-aircraft fire scored a direct hit amidships. A New Zealand pilot, 2nd Lieut. Alfred de Bathe Brandon, of the Royal Flying Corps., who had been shadowing the Zeppelin for over an hour, succeeded in flying above her and dropped a box-full of incendiary darts, further damaging the doomed craft. Three of her gas containers were punctured, she became nose heavy and her commander, Kapitanlieutnant Joachim Breithaupt, jettisoned his remaining cargo of bombs, other equipment and all but four hours-worth of fuel, and headed for the Belgian coast. A radio message was sent for assistance and then the radio was dumped, nevertheless, the craft continued to lose altitude. At 00.15 on 1st April, when down to a height of 500 feet, the hull frame buckled in two places and she fell into the sea about a mile from the Kentish Knock Lightvessel, in the Thames Estuary. The 14 survivors of her crew of 17 were picked up by the armed trawler, *OLIVINE*, and were later transferred to the destroyer, *VULTURE*, which landed them at Chatham dockyard. Two Petty Officers had slashed every gas cell before leaving her but had no other means of furthering her destruction. Other destroyers then arrived on the scene and took her in tow but she sank off Westgate, just to the west of Margate, later that morning; the first Zeppelin to be brought down by gunfire. The recovery of L15 for investigation was a matter of considerable importance and throughout the month numerous attempts were made to salve her. The *GLEN AVON* and *WESTWARD HO* had been moved to Sheerness towards the end of March, and spent the following four weeks in the vicinity of Margate Roads where they assisted in the operation by sweeping a clear seaway for the Zeppelin to be towed into the Thames.

A Rescue Mission and a U-Boat Incident.

At about 10.40 on 26th April 1916 the Dutch cargo steamer, *MAASHAVEN*, was mined 2¾ miles N by W from the North Galloper Lightship. The forward part of the vessel was badly damaged but she remained afloat. The *WESTWARD HO, CAMBRIDGE* and the Thames paddle steamer, *YARMOUTH BELLE*, were at work nearby and rendered prompt and invaluable assistance. The commander of the *CAMBRIDGE*, Lieut. Ralph D. Cooke, stated in his subsequent report:-

> "The Cambridge and Yarmouth Belle were lashed along either side of the
> disabled vessel to steer her, while the Westward Ho towed her, stern first,

towards Harwich. When close to the Sunk Lightvessel the light cruiser, HMS Conquest, and two torpedo boat destroyers steamed close by at full speed, causing a heavy swell which parted all lines and lifted the Cambridge's port sponson over the Maashaven's main rail which was approximately four feet above the water. The engines were immediately stopped but one of the paddle floats came into contact with the ship's side. A boat swung out from the disabled steamer which came into contact with the port forward rail and rigging, the forward gun platform and the anchor davit. The whole of the damage was caused by the swell from the passing flotilla."

Despite the damage the ships arrived safely at Harwich, and following the incident the Commander-in-Chief of The Nore wrote to his counterpart, Commodore R. Y. Tyrwhitt, at Harwich:-

"...The Maashaven was placed in a most favourable position in Harwich to unload her cargo and salve the vessel considering the serious nature of her injuries. The attention of the commanding officers of the 9th and 10th Destroyer Flotillas may be drawn to the disarrangement of the tow and to the damage caused to HMS Cambridge by the wash of the two destroyers escorting HMS Conquest."

Commodore Tyrwhitt replied:-

"...The attention of the officers concerned has been called. The accident is regretted but the ships were ordered to proceed at high speed as a submarine previously reported by the Westward Ho was known to be in the vicinity."

The submarine spotted by the *WESTWARD HO* was UC5, under the command of the particularly audacious Ulrich Mohrbutter. From his base at Zeebrugge he had already penetrated the submarine nets on two previous occasions, in August and November 1915, when he had succeeded in laying mines in the Straits of Dover. His third sortie, however, was to prove unlucky. He had escaped the attentions of the *CONQUEST* and her escorts overnight but on their return to Harwich early on the morning of April 27th 1916, he surfaced in the approaches to the harbour. Several minesweepers were in the vicinity, one of which was the *WESTWARD HO*. Her commander, Lieut. Michael O'Driscoll spotted UC5 again and this time was determined not to let her go. He decided not to attack but to make a nuisance of himself by shadowing the U-boat and foiling her intentions; a plan which proved to be highly successful. In taking avoiding action UC5 ran aground on the Shipwash Shoal, her exact position being 52°03'N, 01°46'E. A summary of her log book for that morning outlines her movements:-

05.15	Dived to avoid minesweepers.
05.30	Came to surface and steered west.
05.40	Boat went violently aground.
	Full speed astern.
	Tide rising. Floated.

06.00	Dived. Trimmed boat.
06.40	Lay on bottom. 16 metres.
09.20	Came up to 9 metres.
11.00	Came to surface.
	Boat ran aground.

By coincidence, HMS *FIREDRAKE*, one of the destroyers attached to the submarine flotilla at Harwich, was exercising in the area at the time. Her commander also spotted the submarine and approached, firing a shot over her conning tower. Her crew were attempting to push her off the shoal with spars but immediately surrendered and were taken prisoner. Over the next couple of weeks the submarine was salved and presented a most unusual sight when, on a fine May morning, with the White Ensign flying above the white, black-crossed emblem of the Imperial German Navy, she was taken into Harwich lashed alongside the *FIREDRAKE*. She was put on to the floating dry-dock off Shotley, her cargo of mines was carefully removed, and she was later put on display to the public at Sheerness. The credit for her capture went to the *FIREDRAKE*, but the officers and crew of the *WESTWARD HO* could feel satisfied that without their initial vigilance and harassing tactics, UC5 may well have slipped away and completed her deadly mission.

The Battle of Jutland.

The U-boat campaign, of a nature somewhat less restricted than that enforced on the commanders in the autumn of the previous year, had been renewed from April 1916, but only temporarily. This, and a number of other factors were combining to force the hand of the High Seas Fleet. In addition to the disastrous German harvest of 1916, Great Britain's distant blockade began to take a firmer hold. Consequently, food shortages became acute and more stringent rationing led to rioting and looting in some cities. The German people were becoming increasingly frustrated at the lack of decisive action by their navy.

Admiral Scheer pressed for the High Seas Fleet to take the offensive by exerting systematic and constant pressure on the Grand Fleet to incite the Admiralty to send out some of its forces; the existing proportions of strength dictating to Admiral Scheer that the Grand Fleet had to be reduced to a size comparable with his own before engaging in full scale conflict.

The High Seas Fleet then began a series of somewhat provocative manoeuvres in the North Sea, and on Tuesday 30th May 1916, it became clear that a large scale move was under way. This time the Admiralty responded to the challenge, in precisely the way which Admiral Scheer feared most; the Grand Fleet sailed, that night, in force! Far out in the North Sea there followed the only large scale encounter of the opposing naval forces in the Great War. The Battle of Jutland was the biggest battle in contemporary naval history, involving 250 ships and 25 admirals, and its result was inconclusive! Although the British losses were higher, both sides claimed victory. It was a considerable blow to British pride, the German fleet had not been destroyed. However, the ships had turned away at the sight of the British Dreadnoughts and never again, in the Great War, were they to attempt another such engagement.

By mid-August most of the damaged German ships had been repaired, but the High

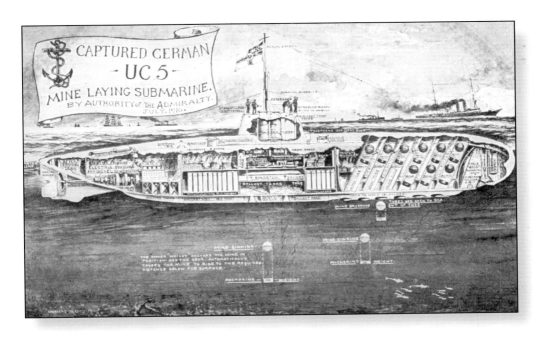

A postcard issued shortly after the capture of submarine UC5. She was on show to journalists at Sheerness on 20th July 1916 and following a press release next day, the public flocked to see her. She was subsequently taken to the USA from Chatham aboard the SS *HELENUS* at the end of September 1916.

Looking every inch a warship! HMS *WESTWARD HO* in the North Sea.

Seas Fleet put to sea only three times after Jutland, and then to little or no purpose. Otherwise, for the rest of the war, the ships lay idle at their moorings in deteriorating condition with their personnel growing increasingly demoralised.

These wider issues of the war, however, were of little concern to the personnel of the minesweepers who continued to pursue, with alacrity, the deadly monotony of their dangerous occupation.

Dover.

For the minesweepers of the Dover Patrol, 1916 was a relatively routine year, which passed without major incident. They continued to sweep ahead of the monitors and destroyers which regularly patrolled the barrage of mines and mine-nets off the French and Belgian coasts.

Commander Walter Rigg, Minesweeping Officer at Dover, reported to his Vice-Admiral on 10th June 1916:-

> "The paddle sweepers at Dunkirk have been employed daily on sweeping the patrol line and since 21st May no German mines have been found. The work of the paddlers has been mostly of a routine nature, enlivened on most days by attacks from hostile aircraft, which on one occasion, realising apparently that only one of the vessels had an anti-aircraft gun, planed down to nearly 1000 feet before dropping its bombs, luckily with no effect. The number of anti-aircraft guns is being gradually increased, when it is hoped that with practise the ships will be able to keep the aircraft at a respectable distance."

Lieut. Alexander Thomson, commander of the Clyde paddler, *DUCHESS OF MONTROSE*, commented:-

> "Nearly every day we would sweep ahead of the monitors to the entrance of the Scheldt. On many occasions our little fleet would consist of three paddlers and the old 'Marshal Soult' or some other monitor equally fast and furious, (about five knots!), and our own escort of destroyers often out of sight on some job or another. Twelve miles away on our starboard beam was Zeebrugge with all the enemy's ultra-modern destroyers. Why the Germans never tried to cut us off is a mystery, it would have been so simple. At times we went along in grand style with our Dover fleet augmented by the fellows from Harwich, and I suppose that kept the enemy guessing."

Lieut. Arthur Edgar Buckland, at one time commander of the *WESTWARD HO*, spent nearly three years in charge of a division of paddle sweepers serving in this area, and his minesweeping diaries record long periods of practically unceasing work. For example, between 21st April and 31st May 1916 his flotilla spent 31 days at sea and steamed 1357 sweeping miles in all weathers.

Even when the ships were in port there was no guarantee of rest for their crews. Capt. Dorling provides a vivid account of life aboard the minesweepers in Dover harbour:-

"The area enclosed by the breakwater may be a haven of refuge, but it is one of the most uncomfortable in the world. In the south and south-easterly gales, even the large destroyers sometimes rolled twenty-five degrees each way while lying at their buoys, so that with the constant movement and the rattle and clatter, sleep was largely a matter of luck, and meals a purgatory...

When I first visited Dover, in a small destroyer, I came to the conclusion that it was the last haven of refuge that the Almighty had ever made.

As for the trawlers and paddlers lying at anchor near the breakwater - they waltzed through half the compass, plunging and surging sickeningly from side to side with their mastheads cutting the wildest capers against the background of a grey sky. Heaven knows how those on board them lived, ate, slept or did anything."

For the *ALBYN*, 1916 was a difficult year during which she experienced a series of accidents and breakdowns, summarised by extracts from her log books:-

"March.

Wednesday 1st	At Blackwall, London, for boiler repairs.
Thursday 2nd	Left dock and anchored off Sheerness.
Friday 3rd	Returned to Dover.
Saturday 11th	Sweeping across the channel and along the French coast-Boulogne to Cap Griz Nez. HMS Jupiter II, (Clyde paddler), disabled while sweeping between Dover and Dungeness, Took her in tow to Dover.
Sunday 26th	While docking at Dunkirk, Lorna Doone, (South Coast paddler), came up and damaged floats of our starboard paddle with her fore-sponson. Albyn swung around damaging rudder and stern post. Remained at Dunkirk for repairs. Entered dry dock at Dunkirk.

April.

Thursday 13th	Out of dry dock,

May.

Monday 8th	Monitor Prince Eugene collided with us while we lay at anchor in Dunkirk Roads, severely damaging port paddle wheel. Engines cannot be used.
Tuesday 9th	Tug Conqueror towed us into Dunkirk Harbour.
Wednesday 10th	Tug Lady Brassey took us in tow for Dover. Depart Dunkirk 08.30, arr Dover 13.40.
Friday 12th	Lady Brassey towed us to buoy off Gravesend.
Saturday 13th	Went into Nelson's Dry Dock, Gravesend.

June.

Friday 2nd	Work completed. Out of dry dock. To anchor off Gravesend.
Saturday 3rd	Anchored off Sheerness to await orders.

Then to Dover to re-commence sweeping between Dover and Dunkirk.

<u>August.</u>

Wednesday 16th   Entered Wellington Dry Dock, Dover, for repairs, after collision with HMS Daisy."

A Commander's Inspection.

As part of his duties as Port Minesweeping Officer at Dover, Commander Rigg was required to carry out regular inspections of the ships and men under his command. Whenever possible he would accompany the ships to sea. One such inspection took place in September 1916 when he took command of HMS *NEPAULIN*, (the Clyde paddle steamer, *NEPTUNE*), and led a flotilla of minesweepers on an exercise. His report to the Vice-Admiral at Dover is quoted in full:-

"I have the honour to report that at 11.30 on 9th September 1916 I proceeded in PMS Nepaulin, accompanied by Glen Avon and Westward Ho, to Dunkirk, arriving there at 16.00, and took under my orders, Balmoral, Ravenswood, Lorna Doone, Jupiter II and Marmion II. The Glen Avon and Westward Ho were lent to this base for the operations embodied in this report. The vessels' commanders were:

No. 584. Jupiter II, Lt. A. E. Buckland RN. (Assistant to MSO, Belgian Coast).
No. 574. Nepaulin, Lt. R. J. Carruthers RNVR.
No. 575. Lorna Doone, Lt. F. A. Robbins RNR.
No. 583. Balmoral, Lt. J. M. Booth RNR.
No. 588. Ravenswood, Lt. B. L. Parker RNR.
No. 586. Marmion II, Lt. G. A. Drummond RNR.
No. 184. Westward Ho, Lt. M. D. O'Driscoll RNR.
No. 185. Glen Avon, Lt. J. Collis Bird RN.

During the operations the patrol line was swept daily by two pairs of paddlers, in accordance with orders from the Commodore. On 11th September I proceeded in Nepaulin at 21.30, under escort, through the West Deep and laid a line of dummy mines in accordance with orders received. During this night run nothing of moment occurred, the whole of the enemy coast being remarkably free from star shells and searchlights.

On 12th September I proceeded in Nepaulin with Westward Ho to investigate the area between the East Breet Bank and the Outer Ratel Bank and found no less than seven British mines in the position it was intended that monitors should work in. As it was evident that one of our lines had been laid ¾ mile out of the charted position, it was decided to abandon the sweep and request further orders. During this operation, when mines were exploding in rapid succession in the sweep, a British sea-plane landed owing to engine trouble and must have experienced a new sensation with mines exploding in very close proximity. The seaplane was towed back to port by the Westward Ho.

Orders were received on Saturday 16th September that operations were completed and the usual patrol was resumed. The Glen Avon and Westward

Ho were then coaled and sent back to Lowestoft.

I beg to bring to your notice Lt. A. E. Buckland RN. This young officer is, in my absence, in charge of the Belgian coast sweepers. I cannot speak too highly of the manner in which he has organised the sweepers or of his untiring energy at all times. He has carried out his work in a highly satisfactory manner.

The Grimsby Paddlers.

The tedious work of sweeping the War Channel off the east coast continued with little incident throughout 1916 until tragedy struck towards the end of the year. At the outbreak of the war a paddle steamer was under construction at the yard of A. & J. Inglis, Glasgow, for the Clyde services of the North British Steam Packet Co. Ltd. Yard No. 309 was launched as the *FAIR MAID*, and on completion of fitting out she was requisitioned by the Admiralty on 7th July 1915 to join the east coast sweeping forces.

On the morning of Thursday 9th November 1916 the *FAIR MAID, DUCHESS OF BUCCLEUCH, DEVONIA* and *CAMBRIDGE* left Lowestoft to carry out a sweep in the war channel off the coast of Norfolk. The *FAIR MAID* and the *CAMBRIDGE* joined sweeps near the Cockle Lightvessel and began sweeping in the direction of the Cross Sands Lightvessel. At 08.15, one mile west of the East Cross Sands buoy, the *FAIR MAID* struck a mine amidships. The whole of the starboard side of the promenade deck was blown away and the after end of the vessel swung clear of the fore part. The *DEVONIA* closed in on her port bow; her commander, Lieut. William V. Rice signalled, "I am going to take you in tow" and several of the *FAIR MAID'S* hands ran forward in order to take a line. Her commander, Lieut. William, "Hurricane Bill", Bayne, hailed the mate of the *DEVONIA* by megaphone and said, "I shall keep afloat for a few minutes, but no longer.", then added almost immediately, "Tell Mr. Rice it's hopeless". It was obvious that his vessel was sinking rapidly and he gave the order to abandon ship.

Boats had been launched from her three consorts which picked up the survivors and transferred them to the *DEVONIA* and *CAMBRIDGE*. Twenty minutes after the explosion the two halves of the *FAIR MAID*, enveloped in steam, sank into the cold waters of the North Sea, as the *DEVONIA* and *CAMBRIDGE* made a speedy return to Lowestoft with her survivors.

The *FAIR MAID'S* second hand, Martin Fielding, described his own experiences:

"I had joined the Fair Maid on 23rd October 1916. We had quite a mixture of merchant seamen and youths who hadn't much sea service. My duties were to rig up the sweeping gear and tend to the paying out of sweep wires on orders from the bridge. I also had to splice all broken ends, and we had plenty!

We were out early one morning and away to the Cross Sands Lightship. While superintending preparations aft I had occasion to admonish one of the seamen for not turning up on time. This led to a bit of cursing and swearing.

The time was about 08.00; then fate took a hand in the argument - just a sort of dull, booming crash, and oblivion as far as I was concerned. When I came to I was underwater, trapped amongst wires and wreckage. I felt as if my lungs would burst but I kicked and struggled, and it seemed an eternity before I reached the surface. How far down I was I don't know, but it seemed a long way. On the surface men were screaming and shouting.

The Fair Maid seemed to be about 100 yards away, almost broken in two but still upright and floating. Boats were being lowered from the Duchess of Buccleuch, the Devonia and other paddlers. I tried to make for the ship, but found I couldn't move my right leg. It was numbed, like cramp; it was freezing at the time and little did I think that I was badly hurt. My eyes were getting dimmed. I was unknowingly bleeding to death.

By a superhuman effort I reached the Fair Maid and grabbing some rope, hauled myself aboard. The man I had been berating for unpunctuality had been killed outright, and his body was lying across the winch. The survivors were soon rescued and I was hauled on board the Devonia, her commander, W. V. Rice, RN., personally tended the wounded, speaking a cheery word to each of us as we sped on our way to hospital at Lowestoft. I had made a rough tourniquet with my tie for my leg. It was severely wounded and the surgeon who stitched me up told me I was lucky I did not bleed to death. The cold water and frost had congealed my blood!"

HMS *DEVONIA* in the Thames estuary.

HMS *GLEN AVON* off the east cost, with the *WESTWARD HO* partally visible in the distance.

HMS *WESTWARD HO* (No. 184), and HMS *CAMBRIDGE* sweeping together. 1916.

BENEATH ARE ALL THE FIENDS

*"Our shallow draught meant that the
torpedoes always went nicely under our
bottom, thank you"*
                        Officer of the *DEVONIA*.

Frustrated by the lack of further action at sea, and in despair of victory on land, Germany returned to its policy of unrestricted submarine warfare on 1st February 1917. The campaign meant that any ships, British, allied or neutral, were liable to be sunk on sight without regard for the lives of their non-combatant crews or passengers. This onslaught on the world's shipping once again incurred the wrath of the United States, this time to such an extent that she entered the war, on 6th April 1917.

Now in possession of 120 U-boats, the German navy was responsible for the torpedoing of several hundred merchant vessels carrying food and munitions to Great Britain, mainly from the United States; the highest number being 430 in April 1917. One out of every four ships that left the British Isles during that month never returned. On 19th April, the worst day of the worst month of the war at sea, eleven British merchant ships and eight fishing craft were destroyed.

From the great increase in the rate of sinkings it appeared more and more likely that the submarines would win the war for Germany. They were being built and sent to sea faster than they could be destroyed. By cutting off the food supplies from overseas the U-boats brought the British Isles ever closer to starvation. Printed on almost every page of the newspapers, the exhortation "Eat less bread", confirmed that Great Britain, at one time, had a mere six weeks supply of corn left. There was also a considerable disruption to the supply of pit props from Norway which adversely affected the coal industry, and which led to the creation of the Forestry Commission, thus ensuring adequate supplies of home-grown timber for the future.

Then, David Lloyd-George, Prime Minister since December 1916, suggested convoys - merchant ships travelling in large groups protected by warships which, by then, had been equipped with hydrophones - listening devices for the detection of submarines, and depth charges - explosive canisters launched from their decks, for their destruction. The Admiralty insisted that the convoy system was quite impracticable but Lloyd-George overruled the experts and proved them wrong. From May 1917, when the convoys began, the number of ships sunk declined rapidly and the number of submarines destroyed rose to an average of nine per month. In addition to unrestricted torpedo attacks there was a huge increase in submarine minelaying. During April 1917, an average of one German mine was laid off the British coast every hour of the day, and each day one minesweeper was lost.

These developments placed additional burdens on the already overtaxed minesweeping service. Most of the mines were laid in the War Channel and drifters provided with wireless were stationed at strategic points to stop all traffic the moment the fairway was found to be so affected. When low water made it unsuitable for sweeping the choice had to be made whether to hold up all traffic, or to risk the sweepers and convoy the vessels through the danger zone. A minefield might be discovered while sweeping was in progress, with the traffic closely following the sweepers. This meant a delay while the merchant ships were made to anchor until the field had been cleared. The usual procedure followed in those instances was to mark the swept channel with small "dan" buoys which were removed immediately after the merchantmen had passed through. Despite these trials and tribulations, record numbers of mines were destroyed.

Re-organisation of the naval staff at the Admiralty towards the end of 1917 greatly assisted operations. In October the overall control of minesweeping became the responsibility of Capt. Lionel Preston, Commander of the Grand Fleet minesweepers since 1914, who was appointed Superintendent, and later Director of the Minesweeping Division, working under the Assistant Chief of Naval Staff. The whole service was therefore co-ordinated under one central control, with excellent results; by the end of the year over 1000 miles of coastal waters in Great Britain and Ireland were being swept each day!

Minesweeping in the North Sea, especially in winter, was no "pleasure cruise" and the paddle steamers took many poundings during the course of their duties. Their decks, so great a source of pride in peace-time, were often ice coated, and to give a foothold to the crew, were sprinkled with ash or sand. This was particularly necessary as the after end was almost denuded of railings and replaced with little more than a wire rope stretched across the stanchions.

In very heavy weather their most vulnerable parts were the paddle wheels, with their numerous radius rods and paddle arms. Great credit was owed to the engineers who, on times, effected repairs under the most dangerous conditions. They worked lashed inside the paddle box, half drowned and with little chance to dodge a charging sea which submerged them, or to escape from a turn of the wheel. Few of these men received decorations for feats which surely deserved them, however, Lieut. John Black, Chief Engineer of the *WESTWARD HO*, was awarded the Distinguished Service Medal for keeping his ship at sea for longer, in the course of a year, than any other paddler.

John Black, a long-serving engineer with P. & A. Campbell Ltd. both before and after the war, had escaped potentially fatal injury earlier during the conflict in an incident mentioned in one of Admiral Charlton's reports to the First Sea Lord:-

> "Near the Swarte Bank a mine exploded under the Westward Ho's stern taking the kite, still attached to its wire, into the air. It described a semi-circle and came down between the paddle boxes. Although it broke through the deck and into the engine room it did not damage the machinery nor the Chief Engineer who was on the platform at the time."

Lieut. G. H. P. Muhlhauser fully appreciated the additional dangers faced by those working "down below" and stated:-

> "The engineers and stokers reported that the explosion of mines was very severely felt in the engine room and the stokehold. Indeed, they often thought that their last moments had come, but the plucky way they carried on during the war was beyond praise. Well they knew that they had not a dog's chance if anything happened, yet they calmly went about their business as if such things as mines and torpedoes did not exist."

With the ships running almost continuously, there was little time for the engineers to carry out essential maintenance. The usual procedure followed by the paddle steamers was to spend about three weeks sweeping daily, followed by three days in port, or in a roadstead, for a tube and boiler clean. In the latter part of the war it was sometimes possible for a two day break after ten days sweeping, but no strict timetable could be followed - the demands of the job were paramount. The ships refuelled as required; the coal was taken from the quaysides, lighters or colliers and unloaded into the chutes leading from the decks into the bunkers. All the men and many of the officers were on hand for this particularly long, tiring and filthy task, which was always followed by a thorough washing down of the ship.

Dover.

While continuing to perform their duties on the French coast with the forces of the Dover Patrol, the minesweepers, including the Dover paddlers, were constantly harassed by enemy aircraft. Their main base, Dunkirk, was situated within twelve miles of the enemy lines and was subject to many air raids. Within one period of two months, 50 air attacks and several long range bombardments took place.

On Sunday 2nd September 1917 several minesweepers were lying alongside the quay at Dunkirk. Between 21.30 and 00.30 an almost continuous air attack took place and a direct hit was scored on the stern of the *ALBYN*. Though severely damaged, she remained afloat, but the fire caused by the explosion was extensive, and only with great difficulty was it eventually put out, with help from the other minesweepers, particularly her Racecourse class consorts, *PLUMPTON* and *LINGFIELD*, even though the latter was badly damaged with over 100 holes in her from aircraft gunfire. The *ALBYN'S* commanding officer, Lieut. C. King, and Second Engineer, B. J. Pearce, were killed and several members of her crew were wounded. Although the after part of the ship was completely burned out and subsequently found to be twisted out of alignment, she was towed across the channel and taken into a Thames shipyard where, during the following six months, she underwent repairs and refitting.

The Grimsby Paddlers.

During the course of 1916, minelaying in the Grimsby area had diminished while that farther north had increased, the enemy now concentrating its activities on the Tyne area. The Grimsby Paddlers had occasionally been required to perform their duties in the war channel off the north-east coast, but early in 1917 their presence in that vicinity was required on a permanent basis and accordingly they were transferred to the River Tyne. From their bases at Jarrow, Wallsend and, occasionally, Hartlepool, they swept northward, towards the Farne Islands, and southward, towards their former base, Grimsby. While on this station the steamers met with one of their consorts from earlier years. The former White Funnel steamer, *LADY MARGARET*, had been sold by P. & A. Campbell Ltd., in 1903, to the Furness Railway, who had used her on their Barrow to Fleetwood service. She had been purchased by the Admiralty in 1908 for use as a tender, being re-named *WANDERER*, but during the course of the war she was pressed into service as a minesweeper under the name of *WARDEN*. The other paddlers already in service on the Tyne were the Clyde steamer, *QUEEN EMPRESS*, the Thames steamer, *WALTON BELLE*, and the Belfast & County Down Railway's, *ERIN'S ISLE*.

HMS *RAVENSWOOD* in the Limehouse Reach, River Thames, in 1917. She is passing the old, long disused, up-river entrance to the West India Dock, and judging by her smart appearance, it appears likely that she is returning to the Dover Patrol following a refit.

PRO Ref: ADM176/1026

The eight ships became known as the "Devonia Unit" and the flotilla gained the distinction of the disposal of the largest number of mines during a single day's sweeping; a fact which is hardly surprising in the light of information which appeared in a minesweeping report of May 1917:-

> "Lieut. Rice, in command of the Devonia Unit, has on many occasions swept with 5 paddlers abreast! Most of the sweeping now done by this unit is carried out in this manner. It would appear that some of the mine mooring wire now used by the enemy is inferior to that previously in use, as on one occasion, when a batch of 8 mines was swept up by using serrated wire, the mooring wire was cut within a minute of being picked up in the sweep."

Lieut. Rice's methods were put to a particularly rigorous test later in the year after an extensive minefield had been laid southward from a position three miles NE of the North Yorkshire coastal village of Skinnigrove. The tug, *BUNTY*, was mined and sunk while towing a small steamer through the area on the evening of 21st October 1917. The Devonia Unit began sweeping early on the following morning and picked up their first mine just inside the war channel, off Whitby. As they made their way down the coast the ships met a northward-bound convoy. Lieut. Rice instructed the commander of the convoy's escort destroyer to signal his charges to steam at slow speed in the wake of the sweepers. By following this procedure the convoy was escorted safely through the danger area, while the paddlers swept up a number of mines which, without doubt, would otherwise have caused the loss of both ships and men. The unit continued to work on the minefield throughout the following two weeks until the area was declared safe. The mines had been laid in batches with a distance of about eight miles between, thus necessitating a considerable amount of sweeping to clear them. Under Lieut. Rice's "Five abreast" system the field was destroyed in remarkably short time.

The Bristol Channel.

During the course of 1917 most of the country's remaining paddle steamers were called up for Admiralty service in an attempt to ease the ever increasing minesweeping burden. The smaller and older vessels, which so far had escaped requisition were pressed into service, even though their capabilities were, perhaps, limited. The last of the White Funnel steamers to be taken over were the *GLEN ROSA* and the *WAVERLEY*, the latter renamed *WAY*, to avoid confusion with the North British Railway's paddler of the same name. Having been repainted at Stothert's Yard, the ships were commissioned on the afternoon of Saturday 26th May 1917; both of them hoisting the White Ensign at 17.00 as they lay in the Cumberland Basin. They sailed from Bristol just after noon on the following Wednesday, the *GLEN ROSA*, (Pendant No.839), under the command of Lieut. John Wooding RNVR. and the *WAY*, (Pendant No.840), under Lieut. Archie Stubbs RNVR. Both vessels carried pilots and shore engineers who were landed at Clevedon Pier, before the ships proceeded to Swansea Bay.

On Friday 1st June they berthed in Milford Haven where sweeping gear was installed to enable them to begin trials about a week later. Their practice sweeps were made along the coast of South Wales between Milford Haven and Swansea Bay and proved to be satisfactory. From mid-June to the end of the month they underwent further refitting at Swansea.

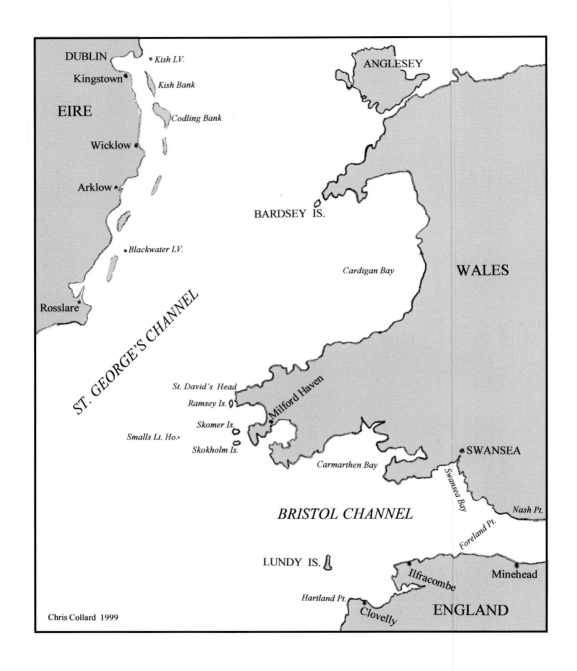

The Bristol Channel and St. George's Channel, showing the principal areas of operations of the Swansea Paddlers.

Their sweeping duties began in earnest on Wednesday 4th July and took them to their main base at Ilfracombe. From there they made occasional sweeps up channel following the coast as far as Minehead, crossing to the Breaksea Lightvessel, then down the Welsh Coast to Swansea Bay before returning to Ilfracombe. Most of their work, however, took them in the opposite direction, on sweeps from Lynmouth Foreland, westward to Bull Point, across Bideford Bay to Hartland Point and beyond, usually as far as Bude but occasionally to Trevose Head. On their return they would often make a detour to the south end of Lundy before returning to Ilfracombe, or anchoring off Clovelly for the night.

By the end of July 1917 they had been joined by two more vessels - Cosens south coast paddle steamer, *MONARCH*, (re-named *MONARCHY*), and the Admiralty paddler, *HARLEQUIN*. The latter vessel was Capt. John Williamson's, *STRATHMORE*, launched in 1897 for service on the Firth of Clyde. She had been purchased by the Admiralty, and renamed *HARLEQUIN*, in 1908, for use as a tender attached to the Naval Dockyards at Chatham and Sheerness. The four steamers formed the unit known as the "Swansea Paddlers", and under the overall command of Lieut. George H. Jenman RNR., of the *MONARCHY* they remained in the Bristol Channel for the duration of the war, apart from one short period which took them farther afield.

The south-east coast of Ireland had become an objective of the minelaying submarines and a flotilla of trawlers had been sent to clear the area. Between Kingstown, (now Dun Laoghaire), and Rosslare are a number of extensive, offshore banks and it was discovered that mines were being laid in the shallow water inside them. Owing to the small range of the tide, of only about three feet, the trawlers were extremely vulnerable and were ordered to discontinue sweeping between the banks and the coast. It was decided that this work could easily and safely be carried out by inshore motor launches, but until an adequate number of those vessels became available, the Swansea Paddlers would replace the trawlers.

The *WAY* and the *GLEN ROSA* made the journey across the St. Georges Channel on Wednesday 1st August 1917, followed by the *HARLEQUIN* and the *MONARCHY* three days later. Using Arklow, Wicklow and Kingstown as their bases, they swept inside the banks between the Blackwater and Kish Lightvessels.

While on the Irish station they may have taken part in deception tactics which were yielding satisfactory results. A Ministry of Information booklet, issued on behalf of the Admiralty in the years after the war, explains:-

> "Off Southern Ireland, the sweepers merely went through the motions of clearing a dangerous area, left it intact, and steamed back to harbour to await the results. It may have been that the senior officer had in mind Psalm 35, verse 8, 'Let destruction come upon him unawares, and his net that he hath laid privily, catch himself, that he may fall into his own mischief.' At all events, it was not long before a U-boat commander arrived on the scene to lay a new consignment.
>
> At 22.30 on Saturday 4th August 1917 his U-boat was blown up by one of the mines from his previously laid field! He was rescued by a Naval patrol and is said to have been highly indignant at the inefficient manner in which the British minesweepers had done their work."

1917.	From		to		, or at	Sea	
			REMARKS		In Company Way		Initials of the Officer of the Watch

Ships clocks put back to G.M.T. at 2 a.m.

In Ilfracombe Harbour

6·35 Cast off & proceeded out of harbour

6·58 Joined up with 840 1½ m. off Capstone. Co. N 79 W. Log 1·8

7·25 a/c. S 74° W. Log 4·9. Bull 20 cables 172°

7·33 a/c. S 62° W. " 6·0

7·41 a/c. S 68° W. " 7·0

9·23 Hartland Pt. abeam 2½ m. Log 19·3

9·26 a/c S 23° W. Log 20·3

9·54 Swept up mine 2½ m. WxS from Hartland Pt. Slipped & destroyed mine. ... 1 mine
Way dropped dan buoy 3·5 m. 239° from Point.

10·45 Rejoined 2 m. W. of Hartland Pt. Co. S 73° W. Log 23·8

10·52 a/c S 23° W.

10·55 Swept up mine on same bearing of Point. ... 1 mine

11·0 Slipped & destroyed mine. Followed Way to Clovelly. Co. as req.

	Noon.			H.W. Dover — 11·40 a.m.		
Latitude		Longitude		.. Ilfracombe — 6·16 a.m. 6·29 p.m.		
D.R.		D.R.				
Obs.		Obs.				

12·24 Hauled in patent log off Clovelly Gallantry Bower showing 38·3

12·30 Anchored off Clovelly in 5 fms. 1½ shackles.

1·30 Weighed & proceeded. following Way. Co. as req. Log 38·3

2·18 Hartland Pt. abeam. Log 47·0

2·35 Joined up 1½ m. W. of Hartland Pt. Co. S 68° W.

2·50 a/c. S 56° W. ... 1 mine

2·55 Swept up mine. WxS from Hartland Pt.

2·57 a/c. N. Log 51·1

3·4 Slipped - Way destroyed mine - 3·50 Rejoined 2 m. W/25 fm Pt.

4·0 Parted - 4·10 Rejoined.

4·20 Swept up mine ... 1 mine

4·27 Swept up mine - slipped & destroyed mines ... 1 mine

5·25 Hartland Pt. abeam 1¾ m. Co. N 69° E Log 65·0

6·37 Rounded Bull Point. Log 79·0. Co. as req. for Ilfracombe.

6·48 Hauled in patent log off Torrs Hill showing 81·0.

7·0 Made fast alongside Way

In Ilfracombe Harbour

A typical day for HMS *GLEN ROSA*, (in company with the *WAY*), in July 1917.

PRO Ref: ADM53/42948

HMS *GLENCROSS* at Ilfracombe.

The Admiralty tender, HMS *HARLEQUIN*.

1917. From *Ilfracombe* to *Arklow*, or at *Sea*

REMARKS	In Company Way.	Initials of the Officer of the Watch

12-30. Take aboard ~~75afms~~ new sweepwire *1 coil ?* In Ilfracombe Harbour

3-0. Cast off & proceed to sea

3-8. Log 0·0 3 cables off Pier. Co. N.W. 33 revs.

6-38. a/c. N14°W. log 40·6 — 6·42 St. Govan L.V. 1 cable to starboard. 4·15

7-30. made number to St. Anne's Head & waited for instructions. hauled in log showing 51·3.

7-50. Proceeded up to Milford, anchoring off harbour at 8·27

10-45. Weighed & proceeded out of harbour

11-24. St Anne's Head abeam ½ m. log 51·2. Co. WNW.

11-45. a/c. NW.

11-53. a/c. NNW.

12-0. a/c. NxW. log 56·9. Skokham L.H. ESE, 1m.

Noon.					H.W. Dover.	10·27 a.m.	10·56 p.m.
Latitude		Longitude			„ Liverpool	10·30 „	10·54 „
°	′	°	′		„ Ilfracombe	4·43 „	5·10 „
D.R.		D.R.			„ St. Anne's Head	3·18 „	3·44 „
Obs.		Obs.					

1-25. Bishop L.H. abeam 4 cables. log 72·3 a/c. N½E.

1-30. „ — „ 19 „ 73·0

4-20. a/c. N4°W. log 101·0

5-0. a/c. N9°W. — 139·4

6-0. „ N12°W — 120·6

6-20. „ N20°W — 124·0

6-34. „ N34°W. — 6·39 ⌁ S. Arklow Bank L.B. Spoke "Sand Duke"

7-25. Proceeded NWxN. log 127·7

7-32. Arklow Bank N°5 buoy log 130·0 a/c NWxN.

8-7. Log hauled in showing 136·5, ½ m. off Arklow.

8-20. Anchored off Arklow harbour, 3 cables E off pier. 5 fms. 2 shackles

The log of the *GLEN ROSA'S* journey to Southern Ireland, Wednesday 1st. August 1917.

PRO Ref: ADM53/42947

Having successfully completed their duties in Ireland, and with the the coastal motor launches arriving much sooner than anticipated, the Swansea Paddlers returned to the Bristol Channel on Monday 13th August. They were joined, on Tuesday 4th September, by a fifth vessel when the Glasgow & South Western Railway's paddle steamer, *GLEN ROSA*, arrived at Swansea. She had been commissioned in mid-July at Liverpool and was re-named *GLENCROSS*. After spending August sweeping in the Firth of Clyde she had journeyed south, via Kingstown and Milford Haven.

Some anxiety was felt by the Admiralty as to the suitability of the smaller, older paddle steamers. The *WAY* and *GLEN ROSA*, for example, had been built for service in the sheltered waters of the Firth of Clyde, the former in 1885 and the latter in 1877. They were now called upon to perform a tough and gruelling job in all weathers, in one of the most treacherous of channels. With the approach of the winter of 1917 the Admiralty called for reports on their progress.

The Senior Naval Officer at Swansea stated that he was, "... very favourably impressed with the five light paddlers and their seagoing qualities. Two were out lately in very severe weather and stood the strain very well". Nevertheless, the ships had been built for summer sailing, and with the onset of winter he suggested that they should be fitted with better weather protection, including the building of wheelhouses on their open bridges, and the installation of slow combustion stoves to provide heating for their accommodation. The Admiralty approved, and also sanctioned the provision of certain "luxury" items: carpets were to be supplied for the officers cabins and the commanders were to have an easy chair and a writing table. From September each of the vessels spent time in dockyard hands for the necessary alterations to be carried out.

Stormy weather.

The winter gales were fast approaching. Ilfracombe was well protected from the prevailing south-westerly winds by the surrounding north Devon hills. However, a strong wind from the north-east would blow straight into the harbour, causing difficulties to ships moored within its limited confines. The first gale from this dangerous quarter was experienced in December 1917 and proved to be exceptionally severe. The *GLEN ROSA* and *GLENCROSS* were not present, the former undergoing repairs in dry dock at Barry and the latter refitting at Swansea, but the other three members of the flotilla rode out the storm under circumstances which were reported to the Admiralty by the Senior Naval Officer at Swansea:-

> "...Owing to the rapid fall of the glass during the night of 15/16 December 1917, Harlequin and Way returned to Ilfracombe early on the morning of the 16th and lay in the outer harbour. There was too much sea at the Stone Bench for any ship to take the ground. At 16.30 matters began to look serious. Harlequin proceeded to the inner harbour and moored alongside Monarchy. At 17.30 the wind and sea had risen to considerable force, the seas breaking over the stone jetty at the entrance to the inner harbour. At 08.00 on Dec 17th the wind backed slightly, cutting down the sea.
>
> Way rode it out in the outer harbour, her CO having taken many mooring precautions and being out of the direct run of the sea. Monarchy and

Harlequin rode well in the inner harbour, stern to the sea. Considering the sea conditions and record force of the gale, damage was slight.

The tides were springs but the north-easterly wind cut down the high water level by about four feet, which eased the situation somewhat."

The above report was accompanied by a plan of Ilfracombe harbour showing the disposition of the ships, and is reproduced below.

The confidence shown in the Swansea paddlers was not misplaced. Their somewhat frail appearance, when compared with their larger and more powerful consorts, disguised a resilience and strength equal to that of the personnel who manned them. Although the area which they patrolled was not heavily mined, and their sweeping quota was comparatively small, they nevertheless performed an invaluable service in ensuring that the sea lanes were kept clear, and their presence gave welcome reassurance to the crews of the many merchant vessels using the Bristol Channel ports.

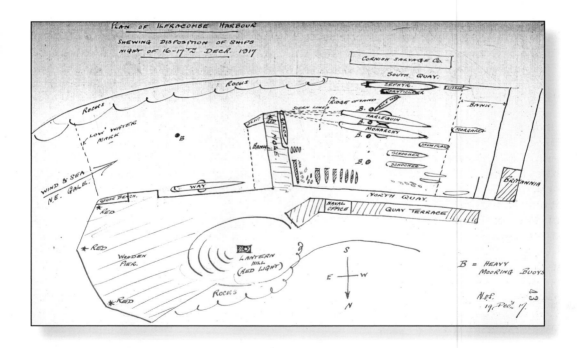

The disposition of ships in Ilfracombe harbour during the severe gale of 16th/17th December 1917.
PRO Ref: ADM137/3055

122

WHEN THE BATTLE'S LOST AND WON

"Our minesweepers were always in action and more than any other type of ship, bore the brunt of the war at sea. We should have been lost without them. All honour to those who swept for mines and lived through those four perilous years to see the hour of their triumph. All honour to those who perished so that the coastwise traffic and fighting ships might pass in safety."
Captain Taprell Dorling, RN. DS0. FR HIST S.

The early part of 1917 had been marked by a large increase in the number of enemy mines destroyed in home waters, which reached its peak in April, when 515 were accounted for. The month of May showed a considerable fall but the April number was again nearly reached in June. From then on there had been, with the exception of September, an almost steady fall, undoubtedly due to the losses of minelaying submarines.

During the course of 1918 the toll of U-boat losses mounted and seriously affected Germany's mine-laying. The total number of allied and neutral merchantmen lost by mines that year fell to twenty-seven. This was brought about, not only by the convoy system, but also by the greater co-operation between the Intelligence and Minesweeping Divisions at the Admiralty, the rapid distribution of information and the firmer control of shipping.

The "Westhope" Enigma.

Something of a mystery concerning the *WESTWARD HO* has arisen from her period with the Devonia Unit; several sources state that she was re-named *WESTHOPE*. The Navy List for the quarter ended 18th June 1918 refers to her by this name but in the next issue, dated 18th September 1918, she is referred to as *WESTERN QUEEN*. Whether, in fact, she was ever known as *WESTHOPE* has always been uncertain; none of her log books from World War One have survived, so the chief source of confirmation is lacking. However, the *WESTWARD HO* and *GLEN AVON* were frequently paired together and from Monday 22nd July 1918 the log book of the latter makes several references to her partner, the *WESTERN QUEEN*. Prior to that date reference was made to the *WESTWARD HO*, but nowhere does the name *WESTHOPE* appear. The mystery, however, is solved by an examination of the Admiralty Weekly Orders: No. 1927, dated 13th June 1918, states, "Westward Ho to be re-named Westhope from 1st July 1918.", but, Weekly Order No. 2091, dated 27th June 1918, states, "Amend new name for Westward Ho to read Western Queen." It is possible that the name *WESTHOPE* was considered and subsequently changed, or it may have been simply an administrative error, but the name was never implemented. The *WESTWARD HO* became *WESTERN QUEEN* from 1st July 1918 and retained that name until the completion of her naval service.

The reason for the change of name is another mystery which can be solved. In the spring of 1918 the Admiralty placed an order with the shipbuilders, White's of Cowes, for four destroyers of the "Modified W Class", one of which, (Yard No. 1543), was to be named *WESTWARD HO*. The paddle steamer was therefore required to relinquish her name in readiness for the new warship. However, the return of peace resulted in a reduction in warship construction and White's order for the four destroyers was subsequently cancelled.

Salvage and Spanish 'Flu.

A minesweeping report issued early in 1918 shows that while minelaying in general was diminishing, that in the Bristol Channel was increasing, and adds:-

> "It would appear that mines in this area are being laid, not in groups, but singly in the main tracks of shipping, particularly in proximity to headlands and lightvessels, for which ships would make."

One such mine was suspected of sinking the British hospital ship, *REWA*, (7308 gross tons), on 4th January 1918, 19 miles $W\frac{1}{4}S$ of Hartland Point. while on passage from Salonika to Avonmouth with 270 wounded soldiers. Miraculously, only four of the ship's complement were lost. It was thought that the mine had been laid close to the point but had drifted farther out on the strong currents and tidal flows around the headland. The Swansea Paddlers were immediately ordered to carry out a thorough sweep of the area, but no mines were found. It was later confirmed, however, that the *REWA* had been sunk by a torpedo from submarine UC55.

The western approaches to the channel were becoming a favorite hunting ground for both the minelaying and torpedo U-boats. During the early hours of Monday 19th August 1918 the Hartland coastguard reported the torpedoing of a steamer off the point. The Clovelly lifeboat immediately put to sea and reached two ship's boats, damaged and full of water, with 25 men, of whom the master was seriously injured. They were taken aboard the lifeboat and the boats were towed back to Clovelly.

Their vessel, the *CHARITY*, of Newcastle, (1735 gross tons), carrying stores for the US Flying Corps in France, was left to her fate. On the same morning the *GLENCROSS*, *HARLEQUIN* and *MONARCHY* left Ilfracombe at 05.00 to sweep an area to the westward. At 06.30, in Bideford Bay, they sighted the wreck of the *CHARITY* drifting up channel. The *GLENCROSS* went alongside, put a towrope aboard and began towing her towards Clovelly. At 07.15 the towrope parted but the crew of the *HARLEQUIN* succeded in putting a line aboard, and with the assistance of the *GLENCROSS* and *MONARCHY*, the wreck was anchored off Clovelly at 11.00. Further orders were requested and at 11.30 the *GLENCROSS*, escorted by her two consorts, began towing the *CHARITY* to Ilfracombe, where they arrived at 17.00. The wreck is believed to have been broken up in Ilfracombe harbour.

The *GLENCROSS* was in the news later that year when she was quarantined in the inner harbour at Ilfracombe from Friday 18th October 1918 for ten days. Nine members of her crew were suffering from influenza; victims of an epidemic of "Spanish 'flu" which swept through England and Wales during late 1918 and early 1919, leaving a death toll of over 110,000 people. The other members of the flotilla appeared to have escaped the worst of the epidemic.

From The Captain of Patrols, Swansea.

To The Director of Minesweeping, Admiralty, S.W.1. (thro'
            The S.N.O., Bristol Channel).

Dated 26th April, 1918.

No. 11/97

    Submitted. In accordance with your Memo BM3.172/2007
of 22/4/18, the following report is forwarded :-

    GENERAL.- Mine Sweeping vessels in this Area sweep
to the Southward of latitude 51.20 N., and so far to the
West as 5° longitude, and South as far as the parallel of
Bude, and to the East of 4° 15' W.

        Milford Haven have taken over the area North
of latitude 51.20 and West of longitude 4.15 W. for
sweeping purposes.

Area swept	Whether daily or periodically.	Number & type of vessels normally employed	Remarks
2' N of Ilfracombe 2' N of Bull Point 2½' N W of Hartland to S.Lundy & back to 3' N of Bull Pt.	Mondays	3 Paddle Mine Sweepers.	See below.
2' N of Ilfracombe 2' N of Bull Point 2½' N W of Hartland 3' W of Bude & back on outside parallel course.	Sundays Tuesdays Wednesdays Thursdays Fridays	- do -	Sweep'rs are varied as circumstances render necessary & also at the discretion of the PMSO.
Ilfracombe - Foreland - Breaksea & back to Ilfracombe.	Saturdays	- do -	- do -

    PADDLE MINE SWEEPERS.- Five in number, work from
Ilfracombe. Three sweep daily, whilst the fourth is in
dock coaling, &c., and the fifth is undergoing repairs.

    I have, since my arrival here, understood that one
Paddle Mine Sweeper has always been in dock for repairs.

A report from the Captain of Patrols outlining the activities of the Swansea Paddlers in the spring of 1918.
PRO Ref: ADM137/3055

Armistice and Surrender.

As the year continued the German U-boat campaign diminished and gradually failed; it ceased altogether on 20th October 1918, and the war at sea was virtually over.

On land the contending armies had moved backwards and forwards on the Western Front, expending millions of lives in the process, but the situation had not changed significantly since 1914. The German High Command realised that the impending arrival of large numbers of American troops in April 1918 would turn the tide against them. Their only hope was to win a decisive victory in France before the American forces arrived. They therefore launched an enormous offensive on the Western Front which met with much initial success. However, lack of reserves made it difficult for the Germans to exploit their breakthrough, and when the Americans appeared in force a mighty allied counter-attack took place. The spent German forces had to retreat and the conflict was almost over.

In October the German Naval High Command prepared for a final "death-ride" against the Grand Fleet but the men of the High Seas Fleet mutinied and the futile operation never took place. The German government appealed for the opening of peace negotiations and the Armistice was eventually signed at 11.00 on 11th November 1918. The Great War had ended.

The internment of the High Seas Fleet was one of the terms of the peace treaty and on 15th November the cruiser, *KONIGSBERG*, brought Rear Admiral Meurer to the Firth of Forth where the details were finalised with Admiral Sir David Beatty, Commander in Chief of the Grand Fleet since 29th November 1916 when Admiral Jellicoe became First Sea Lord. The U-boats were to be surrendered to Admiral Tyrwhitt, at Harwich, and the surface ships to Admiral Beatty in the Forth, en route to Scapa Flow.

On the morning of 21st November ships of the Grand Fleet, under Admiral Beatty in HMS *QUEEN ELIZABETH,* sailed from Rosyth to a position 40 miles east of May Island to encircle the High Seas Fleet and bring its ships to anchor in the Firth of Forth. The Grand Fleet ships took up their positions in the open sea in two columns in single line ahead. Suspicious of a last minute strike, the British ships were at action stations but as time passed the tension eased. The Forth was full of small craft packed with journalists and sightseers, including the *GLEN USK*, carrying a party of about 1000 schoolchildren from Granton to witness the event. The fleet which Beatty saw, manned by its mutinous crews, was so different from that which he had encountered at Jutland. The only major battle of the war resulted in stalemate but there is little doubt that the Battle of the Skaggerak, as it is known to the German people, set the High Seas Fleet on the downward path to demoralisation and decay.

By 27th November the fleet was safely interned at Scapa Flow and while the ships rusted at anchor, the allied politicians and admirals argued over what to do with them. However, their deliberations were cut short on 21st June 1919 when, in a final gesture of defiance, the ships were scuttled and all but one of the battleships sank or were beached. The High Seas Fleet passed into the chronicles of history.

Mine Clearance.

At the beginning of the war the regular minesweeping force had consisted of six old torpedo-gunboats. At its end it embodied 726 vessels of various types. 214 minesweepers had been sunk during the 4 years, 3 months and 7 days of hostilities, approximately one per week. When the Armistice came and men's thoughts turned to peace, demobilisation and finding a job, the minesweepers' work was still not finished. For them there remained the post war task of mine clearance - an infinitely more dangerous operation.

For as long as the conflict had continued the war channels had been kept clear, but what dangers now lurked outside the carefully swept sea-lanes by way of uncharted enemy minefields and mines laid at random? Additionally, there were the allied minefields; the clearance of all those deadly devices of destruction was imperative.

The matter had been considered before the war had ended and it was decided that the allied powers should be responsible for sweeping specific sea areas and to collect and co-ordinate the results of the work as it went on in order to publish periodical reports of progress for the benefit of worldwide shipping. Great Britain was responsible for a large part of the North Sea, and in February 1919 the Mine Clearance Service was established under the direction of Capt. Lionel Preston. There were special rates of pay for the 18,000 personnel of this voluntary service; an extra £2 2s per week was paid in addition to the normal service pay plus a bonus of £5 5s for each German mine and £1 1s for each allied mine swept up. At the time of the Armistice the *WAY* and *GLEN ROSA* were in dry dock, the former at Bristol and the latter at Swansea. Their work in the Bristol Channel was over but on leaving the dry docks they were held in reserve, like their consorts, and by Monday 6th January 1919 the five Swansea Paddlers were laid up at Ilfracombe. A week later they were on the move again, bound for Sheerness and the task of mine clearance. The night of Friday 24th January found the *WAY* and *GLEN ROSA* lying alongside the South Parade Pier at Southsea. Although neither vessel would sail on civilian service again, their call at the south coast resort was seen as a portent of happier days to come. After coaling at Dover the two ships arrived at Sheerness on the afternoon of Monday 27th January. There they joined the White Funnel steamers of the Devonia Unit, which had previously sailed south from the Tyne, and began sweeping their allocated sector, the Thames Estuary. The *BRITAIN* and *GLEN USK*, in the Firth of Forth, were similarly employed.

At Dover, however, the *ALBYN*, having returned to Dunkirk on 1st March 1918 on completion of her lengthy refit following her bombing, was temporarily laid up with boiler trouble. The *RAVENSWOOD* was also out of action owing to a rudder defect. Neither ship, therefore, was able to participate in the mine clearance operations.

At the board meeting of P. & A. Campbell Ltd, on Friday 13th December 1918, it had been carried, on Capt. Alec's advice, that in view of the additional risks soon to be incurred by the minesweepers, an additional insurance cover of £5000 per vessel should be sought. Fortunately, none of the fleet sustained mine damage but on the evening of Monday 10th February 1919 the steamer, *J. E. O'NEILL*, rammed the *GLEN AVON* in the Thames estuary. She sliced into the after end of her starboard sponson, severely damaging the paddle box and paddle wheel. The *GLEN AVON* was towed into Sheerness and was subsequently out of action.

The enormous task of mine clearance was nearing completion in November 1919, when the service was disbanded but minesweeping, on a reduced scale continued, and not until the summer of 1921 was the North Sea fully cleared of mines. However, the hired paddle steamers were gradually released by the Admiralty and returned to their companies.

Returning Home.

The White Funnel steamers were relieved of their duties early in 1919. All that had been required of them had been gallantly done. What adventures had befallen them since they last saw their home port - bombings, torpedoings and enemy fire; shakings from mines and depth charges; sweeping gear blown out of the water to crash on their decks; stubborn mines entangled in their sweeps having to be cut away with hammer and chisel; skirmishes with U-boats; intense cold and savage winter gales - they had come through it all! Two did not return, but their share of triumph was borne by their consorts as they came back, one by one, to Bristol.

The following details of their homeward journeys, unfortunately incomplete, are all that appear in the company's memorandum book:

"ALBYN

February 1919.

Tuesday 11th	Left Dover.
Thursday 13th	At Falmouth, coaling.
Saturday 15th	Arrived at Bristol at 19.45.

RAVENSWOOD

February 1919.

Friday 14th	Left Dover in tow of *LORNA DOONE*.
Monday 17th	Sheltering in Brixham Harbour.
Friday 21st	Sheltering in Falmouth Harbour.

March 1919.

Monday 3rd	Left Falmouth.
Wednesday 5th	Arrived at Bristol at 09.15."

The Dover Patrol records state that the *RAVENSWOOD'S* steering gear and rudder were defective. She had been out of action since early February 1919 and was unable to return to Bristol under her own steam. After she had been assisted into the Straits of Dover by the *LORNA DOONE* the tow was taken over by an unidentified Admiralty tug. The *RAVENSWOOD* entered Hill's Dry Dock at Bristol on Thursday 6th March and was officially returned to P. & A. Campbell Ltd. on Thursday 28th March 1919; two days after leaving dry dock, following extensive repairs carried out at the expense of the Admiralty.

"GLEN AVON

March 1919.

Friday 7th — Left Sheerness in tow of HM tug *ST. BEES.*
Tuesday 11th — Arrived at Bristol at 14.45.
Wednesday 26th — Left Bristol at 12.50 in tow of tugs *BELLE* and *SEA QUEEN* to Kingroad, (off Portishead). Then in tow of HM tug *ROLL CALL* for Troon.
Saturday 29th — Arrived at Troon at 08.30.

WAY

March 1919.

Friday 14th — Left Sheerness at 05.00 for Portland. Arrived at Portland at 22.00.
Saturday 15th — Coaled and left Portland at 13.15.
Sunday 16th — Anchored off Ilfracombe at 08.40.
Monday 17th — 03.00 Hove up anchor and proceeded. Arrived at Bristol at 09.00.

GLEN ROSA

March 1919.

Tuesday 18th — Left Sheerness at 09.00.
Wednesday 19th — Arrived at Portland for coal.
Thursday 20th — Left Portland at 15.30. Anchored off Torquay for shelter at 20.15.
Friday 21st — Hove up and proceeded at 05.00. Passed Eddystone at 09.10 Arrived at Falmouth at 12.20.
Saturday 22nd — Left Falmouth at 05.00. Arrived at Ilfracombe at 17.40.
Sunday 23rd — Left Ilfracombe at 05.00. Arrived at Bristol at 10.30.

WESTERN QUEEN

March 1919.

Thursday 27th — Left Sheerness and anchored off Eastbourne.
Friday 28th — Left anchorage, proceeded to off Weymouth.
Saturday 29th — Left anchorage off Weymouth.
Sunday 30th — Arrived at Falmouth.
Monday 31st — Left Falmouth at 06.30. Anchored in Walton Bay, (near Clevedon), at 20.00.

April 1919.

Tuesday 1st — Arrived at Bristol at 08.00.

BRITAIN

March 1919.

Monday 31st	Left Granton, Firth of Forth.
April 1919	
Friday 4th	At Portree, Isle of Skye.
Saturday 5th	At Oban.
Tuesday 8th	Arrived at Glasgow.

GLEN USK

March 1919.

Monday 31st	Left Granton, Firth of Forth.
April 1919	
Tuesday 8th	At Stornoway, Isle of Lewis.
Friday 11th	Arrived at Glasgow.

DEVONIA

April 1919

Wednesday 30th	Left Sheerness.
May 1919.	
Thursday 1st	Left Portland.
Friday 2nd	Arrived at Bristol at 21.45."

CAMBRIDGE

April 1919

Tuesday 29th	Left Sheerness.
May 1919.	
Thursday 1st	At Devonport.
Saturday 3rd	Left Portland.
Sunday 4th	Arrived at Bristol at 10.30.

Some of the steamers underwent their refits elsewhere, but most of them sailed up the River Avon unheralded and unsung and slipped quietly into Bristol's Floating Harbour; not a heroes welcome perhaps, but many people breathed a sigh of relief. In the uncertain aftermath of "The War to end all Wars", it was good to see them home!

To quote Capt. Taprell Dorling once more:-

"The mine menace no longer exists. Ships can pass on the sea and along the coastwise traffic routes without the constant fear of the sudden, underwater explosion which may send them reeling to the bottom...

Remember the minesweepers. They helped to make history. Remember too that they were manned for the greater part by officers and men of our Merchant Navy and Fishing Fleets, officers and men of the Royal Naval Volunteer Reserve, and civilians who had never been to sea before the outbreak of the hostilities - all of whom flocked to enrol themselves for this hazardous service when the call came."

The Swansea Paddlers laid up at Ilfracombe in January 1919 - a "confusion" of funnels and masts. The ships are, (from left to right), HMS *GLENCROSS*, HMS *MONARCHY*, HMS *HARLEQUIN*, HMS *GLEN ROSA* and HMS *WAY*.
(Gratton Phillipse)

Home again! HMS *ALBYN* leaving the Cumberland Basin to enter Hill's dry dock on the morning of Monday 17th February 1919. She was officially handed over by the Admiralty to P. & A. Campbell Ltd. at noon on Saturday 15th March 1919.

HMS *RAVENSWOOD* at the Mardyke Wharf, Bristol, on Wednesday 5th March 1919, after being towed from Dover by an Admiralty tug. She is flying her long, white paying-off pendant from her foremast. The pendant, which signified that a ship's naval service had been completed, varied in length according to the length of service of the vessel: the longer her service, the longer her pendant.

HMS *GLEN AVON*, returning to Bristol in tow. Tuesday 11th March 1919.

HMS *GLEN AVON*, laid up at the Mardyke Wharf, Bristol, in March 1919.

HMS *WAY* returns to Bristol on Monday 17th March 1919.

HMS *GLEN ROSA* arriving at Bristol, Sunday 23rd March 1919.

HMS *WESTERN QUEEN* arriving at Bristol, Tuesday 1st April 1919. A note in the company's memorandum book for 20th May 1919 states: "Westward Ho, Glen Rosa and Waverley, hire ceases from Admiralty this day pm."

HMS *DEVONIA* in the Cumberland Basin, Saturday 3rd May 1919; the day after she arrived at Bristol from Sheerness.

HMS *CAMBRIDGE* arriving at Bristol, Sunday 4th May 1919.

The *WAVERLEY*, de-commissioned and laid up at Bristol in 1919.

The *GLEN AVON*, on arrival at Troon on Saturday 29th March 1919, showing the extensive damage to her starboard sponson, paddle and paddlebox, caused by her collision with the SS *J. E. O'NEILL* in the Thames estuary.

ALARUMS AND EXCURSIONS

"The forcing of the Dardanelles would have shortened the war by two years, and spared millions of lives."
Sir Roger Keyes. Commodore, Eastern Mediterranean.

"Damn the Dardanelles. They will be our grave".
First Sea Lord, Sir John Fisher, in a letter to Winston Churchill. April 5th 1915.

The *BARRY* was the only White Funnel steamer not employed as a minesweeper during the Great War. She was, however, the first member of the fleet to take up duties outside her civilian role. She finished her season on Friday 14th August 1914, and exactly a week later embarked 400 German prisoners of war, together with an escort of 200 men of the Royal Scots, from the Hain Steamship Co's, *TREVILLEY*, at anchor in Walton Bay. The prisoners of war were disembarked at Dublin on Saturday 22nd August. The *BARRY* remained at Dublin overnight and on the following day she shipped a large number of civilian prisoners who were landed at Douglas, Isle of Man, at 06.00 on Monday 24th. Sailing from Douglas at 08.30 on the same morning, she returned to Bristol, where she arrived on Tuesday 25th, disembarking the escort at Hotwells Landing Stage and docking in the Cumberland Basin before being laid up in the floating harbour.

On Monday 14th December 1914 she was hired by the Admiralty, at a cost of £35 per day, to act as a patrol vessel in the Bristol Channel. She worked from Barry with a double crew of P. & A. Campbell officers and men, working seven days on and seven off. Her masters during this period were Capt. J. H. Denman and Capt. Daniel Ryan, with Chief Engineers John Black and Robert Wilson.

These duties were interrupted on Friday 5th March 1915 when she was ordered to attend the P. & O. liner, *DONGOLA*, then acting as a troopship, off Barry. The *DONGOLA* had left Avonmouth that morning with 1000 men of the Border Regiment, bound for Egypt, but had collided with her escort and was unable to proceed. The *BARRY* disembarked the soldiers, landing 500 at Barry and 500 at Cardiff, after which she resumed her patrol work.

At the P. & A. Campbell board meeting on Monday 10th May 1915, the Secretary reported that notice had been received from the Severn Defences Authority to terminate the agreement for the hire of the *BARRY*. Her duties were completed on the morning of Saturday 22nd May, after which she sailed to Bristol to lay up at the Mardyke Wharf.

Farther afield.

Early in 1915, in the hope of breaking the deadlock of trench warfare on the Western Front, Winston Churchill suggested taking steps to remove Turkey from the war. He proposed that the Royal Navy should sail through the Dardanelles - the narrow stretch of water which led from the Eastern Mediterranean towards the Black Sea. This

The Cumberland Basin, Bristol, at 09.30 on Tuesday 25th August 1914. The *BARRY*, (left), returning fro

visit to Ireland and the Isle of Man, passes HMS *DEVONIA*, preparing to leave for mine sweeping trials.

would be the first stage in the passage of the fleet through the minefields and past the guns of the coastal defences, into the Sea of Marmora; the landing of the army on the Gallipoli peninsula being another step to the eventual goal - the capture of Constantinople. Its possession, combined with the command of the Sea of Marmora and the occupation of Gallipoli, would cut Turkey's communication with Europe. It would then be possible to ship war equipment to Russia all the year round by way of the Black Sea ports, her northern ports often being icebound; and so, with her huge manpower, she would be of immense assistance to the allied cause. The proposals were backed by the Greek Government, under its Prime Minister, Eleutherios Venizelos, who, in August 1914, had placed the full military resources of Greece at the disposal of the Triple Entente of Great Britain, France and Russia. Many people considered the Gallipoli campaign an ill-considered side show, but others saw it as a sound and far-sighted conception that might well alter the course of the war.

Controversy about the campaign continues to this day but most authorities now agree that its failure was primarily due to the abortive naval efforts to force the Dardanelles during February and March 1915, which gave the Turks ample warning that landing was intended. Over a month elapsed before the army was ready to land on April 25th 1915, and by that time, the Turkish forces had been strengthened and they were in a position to bring the advance to a standstill. The only chance of success then lay in substantial reinforcements being deployed at once. However, the decision to undertake large military commitments in the Eastern Mediterranean was half-hearted, owing to the huge demand for manpower on the Western Front. Nevertheless, a further offensive was planned for August. Reinforcements of all kinds were required - men, materials and additional ships to carry them.

In Bristol, on Wednesday 30th June 1915 the *BARRY* was requisitioned by the Admiralty, and two weeks later she began taking on a considerable quantity of supplies. From the amount of coal which was loaded it became apparent that she was to undertake a long voyage; her bunkers were filled to their capacity of about 30 tons and a similar amount was stowed in baskets around the main deck. Her officers and crew had been signed on at the following rates of pay :-

Master	- £25 per month plus 15% less 2/- per day for food
Mate	- £15 " " " " " " " " " "
2nd. Mate	- £12 " " " " " " " " " "
Ch. Engineer	- £24 " " " " " " " " " "
2nd. Engineer	- £15 " " " " " " " " " "
3rd. Engineer	- £12 " " " " " " " " " "
Ch. Steward	- £12 " " " " including food
Asst. Steward	- £8 " " " " " "
Cook	- £10 " " " " " "
10 sailors	- £8 " " " " " "
9 firemen	- £8 " " " " " "
3 trimmers	- £8 10s 0d" " " " " "

The Guardian of the Bristol Channel - Lundy from the north-west. For the personnel of HMS *BARRY*, bound for the Eastern Mediterranean, this would have been their last sight of British shores for two years.

The *BARRY* left Hotwells Landing Stage on the afternoon of Saturday 24th July and anchored off Penarth overnight, waiting for her cook, who had "jumped ship" and was under arrest in Bristol. The cook arrived on board at 04.30 next day, under escort, after which the *BARRY* weighed anchor and proceeded down channel. A few hours later the Chief Engineer reported to her Commander, W. H. Venning, that the high pressure cylinder cover was blowing with a considerable loss of steam, and at 09.00 she put into Ilfracombe for repairs. At 15.10 that afternoon she was ready to continue her journey and sailed north-westward, it has been said, under sealed orders, although there is no evidence in confirmation of this point. Her destination, however, was the Eastern Mediterranean, where she was to play her part in the Dardanelles campaign!

Her log book for the outward journey is quoted here with slight editions; the letters in brackets refer to the approximate positions on the maps on pages 146 and 147.

"Sunday 25th July 1915.

15.10	Dep. Ilfracombe. Streamed log.
17.50	Lundy Island bearing SE½E. 11 miles. Log 34 miles. (A).
	Altered course to S87°W Magnetic.
20.10	Lat. 51°10 N. Long. 5°40 W. Log 68 miles. (B)
	Altered course to W Magnetic.
24.00	Wind freshening. Strong breeze. Rising sea. Log 112 miles.

Monday 26th July 1915.

12.00	Heavy head sea. Course W.
	Lat. 50°11 N. Long. 9° 54 W. Log 243 miles. (C).
15.00	Lat. 50°N. Long 10°40 W. Log 269 miles. (D)
	Altered course to S22°W.

Tuesday 27th July 1915.

12.00	Weather moderating.
	Lat. 45°28 N. Long. 11°7 W. Log 552 miles. (E).
20.00	Engineer reported insufficient coal to reach Oporto,
	About 3 tons left.
	Altered course to S48°E Magnetic to reach Corcubion.

Wednesday 28th July 1915.

07.35	Passed Cape Finisterre, 1½ miles, then proceeded to Corcubion.
08.00	Proceeded to coal.
17.00	Hove up and proceeded down bay.
17.09	Lobeira Grande abeam. Set course SW. Reset log.

Thursday 29th July 1915.

12.00	Lat. 39°20 N. Long. 10°4 W. (F).

Friday 30th July 1915.

12.00	Lat. 36°2 N. Long. 7°11 W. (G)
19.15	Took pilot aboard - moored in Gibraltar.

Saturday 31st July 1915.
12.05   Left wharf at Gibraltar. Reset log. Course E.

Sunday August 1st 1915.
18.00   Took pilot aboard at Cap Caxine to enter Algiers.

Monday 2nd August 1915.
15.30   Left Algiers. Reset log.

Wednesday 4th August 1915.
10.20   Moored at Valletta Harbour, Malta.

Thursday 5th August 1915.
10.05   Left Valletta Harbour. Set log. Courses SE/E to E$\frac{1}{2}$S.

Friday 6th August 1915.
12.00   Heavy sea. Indirect courses followed.
               Weather moderated later in the day. Course NE$\frac{1}{2}$E.
21.47   Ovo Island abeam.
23.35   Cape Malea abeam.

Saturday 7th August 1915.
03.00   Anti Milos abeam.
08.10   Livadia Point, (Tinos), abeam. Altered course to N.
12.43   Psara, (N. end), abeam."

At 18.00 she passed Kombi Island, at the entrance to Mudros Bay on the island of Lemnos, one of the islands placed at the disposal of the allies by the Greek government. The Gallipoli invasion force had assembled in Mudros Harbour earlier in the year, prior to its initial landings, with subsidiary bases on Imbros, Tenedos and Skyros. The sight which greeted the *BARRY* was one of contrasts. The island was hilly but almost bare of trees because of the fierce winter winds that sweep across from the Dardanelles; in the distance ancient windmills bore witness to the island's small population ekeing out its existence from the barren soil. Below stood the contemporary face of warfare - row upon row of tents and huts which housed the troops, and in the huge natural harbour of Mudros Bay, troopships, hospital ships, supply ships and warships: as the poet, John Masefield, who was present at the campaign, described it, "Ships, more ships, perhaps, than any port of modern times has known; they seemed like half the ships of the world." Amid this vast armada the *BARRY* took her place as a supply ship.

The remoteness of the Gallipoli Peninsula presented extreme difficulties in providing the land-based troops with even the basic necessities of life. The only other base that could be used, apart from Mudros Bay, was Kephalo Harbour on the neighbouring island of Imbros, but neither had any piers, jetties, or warehouses. Everything that the army needed had to be ferried ashore from the large supply ships, operating from the main base at Alexandria, 800 miles away, by smaller vessels and landed at the makeshift piers on the beaches. The supply services frequently had to be carried out, not only under adverse weather conditions, but also under fire from the

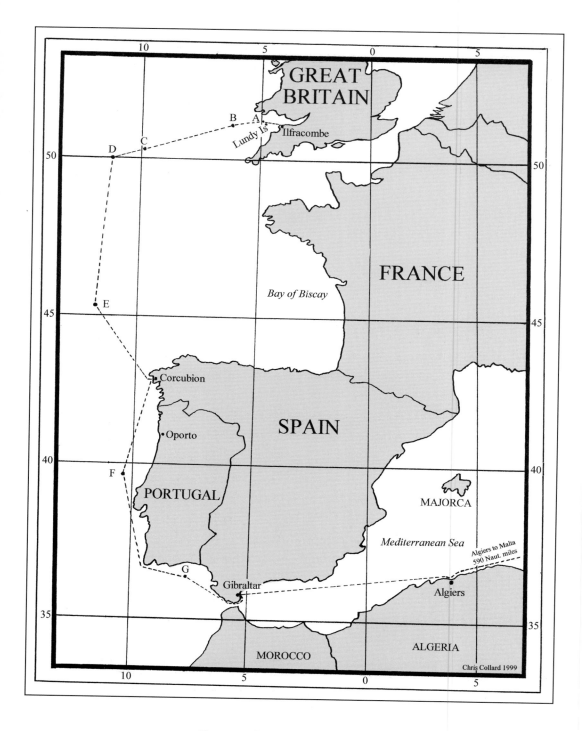

The outward journey of HMS *BARRY*.

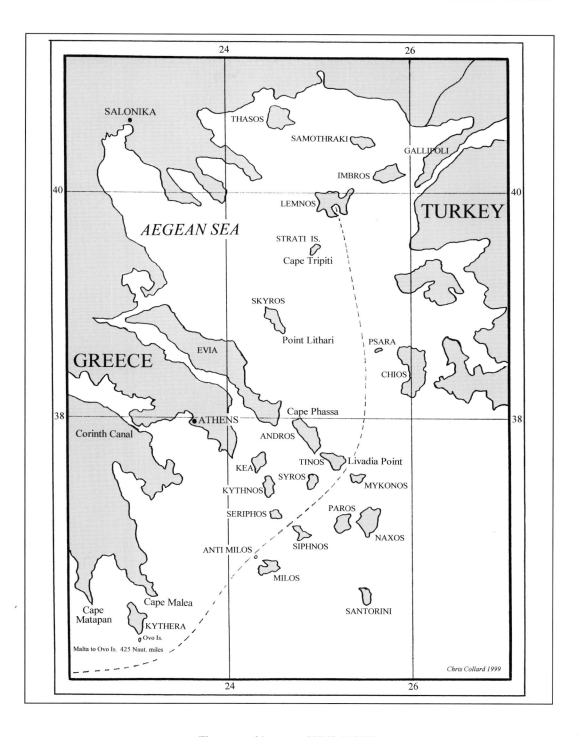

The outward journey of HMS *BARRY*.

Turkish shore batteries. On Monday 9th August the Barry took her first cargo of supplies from Mudros to Suvla Bay. The Bristol Channel and District Guide of 1920 states:

> "There she received her baptism of fire, as troops and ammunition were landed under shell fire from the hills of Suvla Ridge....... and though missiles fell on both sides, the Barry was never once hit. Her first trip successfully completed, she was away again for reinforcements and food for our guns".

Then came a mishap which put the Barry out of commission for a time. On the evening of Wednesday 18th August, having just loaded with coal and sundries for Suvla Bay, she collided with the armed boarding steamer, *WHITBY ABBEY*, in Mudros Bay and sustained such damage to her stern that she was unable to proceed to sea. Her cargo was transferred to another steamer and the *BARRY* moored alongside the repair ship, HMS *RELIANCE*. There she remained until Wednesday 1st September when, her damage made good, she was able to return to her former duties carrying men, ammunition, mail and all manner of supplies from Lemnos to the mainland. To quote the Bristol Channel and District Guide once again:-

> "During these trips she visited Anzac Cove as well as Suvla Bay, usually doing two journeys a day...
> She was constantly under fire and although shells splashed in the water alongside her, she seemed to bear a charmed life, for never once was she struck. What this means may be gathered from the fact that each trip from the torpedo nets at Mudros Bay to Suvla was something like 60 miles and had to be done on a set course because of the minefields."

The August offensive reached stalemate by the middle of the month, like that of the previous April, as a consequence of too few troops to gain a foothold on the peninsula, and in any case, the Turks were waiting; the vital element of surprise had been lost. More allied troops were demanded but were not forthcoming as all available manpower was required for the offensive planned for the Western Front in September.

At home controversy raged within the government about the continuation of the Gallipoli campaign. In October the Chief of the Imperial General Staff, Lord Kitchener, wavered over the question of evacuation. Some planning for the possibility of a winter campaign took place with stores and equipment being amassed to build up a reserve against bad weather. However, in October Kitchener visited the Gallipoli peninsula. The state of the demoralised troops shocked him. They lived in total squalor which resulted in a sick list almost as long as the casualty list in battle. He reluctantly ordered plans to be drawn up for the evacuation of Anzac Cove and Suvla Bay, the occupation of Helles Beach continuing for the time being.

On his return to London in late November he found that circumstances had changed; Winston Churchill had resigned and Sir William Robertson had all but replaced Kitchener as Commander of the Imperial General Staff. It was Robertson who decided that enough was enough, and ordered the complete abandonment of the Gallipoli campaign and the re-direction of the remaining troops to the Western Front.

By a most unusual quirk of fate the weather then played an unexpected and violent hand. During the first few weeks of November a series of gales damaged beach installations and meant a busy time for the *BARRY* and other supply ships delivering materials for their repair. Then, on the night of Friday 26th November violent thunderstorms and a SE gale raged over the peninsula, followed by 24 hours of torrential rain which caused severe flooding. Suvla Bay was the worst hit; most parts of the front were exposed, and many of the trenches were dug into flat, low-lying ground or in dried up water courses. Within a few hours the deluge had swept through them and carried many British and Turkish soldiers to their deaths. But this was merely a prelude. The wind then veered to the north and increased to hurricane force, bringing with it snow and icy sleet; conditions which were almost unheard of in November.

The soldiers, as yet without winter kit, wrapped themselves in sodden blankets. At night the temperature plummeted and the cold was intense: sentries were found at daybreak, still standing at their posts with their rifles in their hands, frozen to death. The impact of the Gallipoli blizzard lay in its suddenness and its severity. It was the worst for 40 years, the weather experts had not expected it, and no one was prepared for it. Throughout the duration of the blizzard the *BARRY* carried out her duties despite the atrocious conditions. On the night of Thursday 25th November she had lain at anchor in Mudros Bay. Her log book for the following four days, slightly edited, continues:-

> "Friday 26th November 1915.
>
> | | |
> |---|---|
> | 06.55 | Hove up anchor. |
> | 07.03 | Made fast alongside "Moyner". Loaded sandbags. |
> | 10.55 | Cast off and made fast alongside "Anwick Castle". Loaded mail. |
> | 11.45 | Left "Anwick Castle" and dropped anchor. |
> | 14.20 | Hove up and proceeded alongside "Aragon". Loaded packages. |
> | 16.05 | Left "Aragon". |
> | 16.20 | Cleared boom. |
> | 16.40 | Eased down to secure anchor. Rough sea. Ship labouring and straining badly. Decks leaking fore and aft. |
> | 17.15 | Cape Irene abeam. |
> | 20.30 | Kephalo abeam. |
> | 22.10 | Entered outer nets at Suvla and anchored. Weather too rough to discharge. Strong wind with rough sea. Overcast |
>
> Saturday 27th November 1915.
>
> | | |
> |---|---|
> | 07.30 | Hove up and proceeded in. Made fast alongside hulk, commenced discharging. |
> | 10.30 | Finished discharging and commenced loading. |
> | 12.00 | Finished loading. Ship delayed waiting for troops. Strong wind with heavy squalls. Dull, overcast, raining. Troops cancelled. |
> | 18.00 | Let go from hulk. Anchored, port and starboard. |

| 18.45 | Ship dragging. Hove up, proceeded closer in. Dropped anchors again. |
| 20.00 | Wind continuing with violent squalls. Raining heavily, black and stormy. |

Sunday 28th November 1915.

04.00	Violent gale blowing. Thick, dirty weather. Ship ranging heavily.
08.00	Gale increasing in violence. Raining and light snow showers. High sea breaking on point.
17.30	HMS Folkestone anchored giving us a foul berth. While heaving up, sheered and drove down on her smashing us badly on the bow and starboard side upperworks. Ship leaking forward. Cemented up stem block stopping leak considerably.
24.00	Gale continuing. Light snow showers with driving sleet.

Monday 29th November 1915.

01.00	Gale increasing. High sea. Ship sheering badly.
02.00	Ship started dragging close down on store ship S58. Manoeuvred clear with engines.
04.00	Gale moderating slightly. Still high sea. Heavy rain and sleet. Heavy squalls. Dull and overcast.
12.00	Had various attempts to heave up anchor. Both anchors had fouled S58's cables. Ship hove up tight on cables.
13.00	Ship dragging down on S58. Slipped both anchors and buoyed cables.
13.30	Arrived alongside hulk, embarking sick.
14.30	Left Suvla.
19.30	Made fast alongside "Umsinger" in Mudros Bay."

By Tuesday 30th November, when the wind abated, the allied army had lost one tenth of its strength - 200 men had been drowned, 5000 were suffering from frostbite and a further 5000 were casualties from a variety of other causes.

The *BARRY* cast off from the *UMSINGER* on the 30th and made fast alongside the *ARAGON* to unload "transit stores". (The *ARAGON* was the passenger liner requisitioned from the Royal Mail Line at a cost of £300 per day, which was used as a communications vessel and acted as the headquarters of the supply operations). The *BARRY* was then employed in transporting casualties from Suvla Bay. The naval captain who superintended the operation ordered a number of small steamers to be sunk for use as a breakwater on to which gangways were placed to help the men aboard, many of whom could scarcely walk. The soldiers were transferred in this manner into lighters which then took them to the hospital ships in Mudros Bay.

She then continued running between Mudros and Suvla Bays with supplies until the beginning of the withdrawal from Gallipoli. The major part of the evacuation of Suvla Bay and Anzac beach took place on the nights of Saturday and Sunday 18th and

LOG of the S.S. *Barry* from *Bristol* to *Admiralty Service*

Hours.	Courses.	Speed.	Wind.	*Friday* REMARKS. 3rd *December*
7·0 AM				Hove up anchor. 8·0 Made fast alongside
				"Gibralter" loaded oil etc .
8·0 „			Various	Light airs, fine clear. Bar 29·88
NOON				Finished loading. 1·45 pm Cast off
2·0 PM				Made fast to "Aragon" loaded parcels
				& Mail. Troops sent in tug
4·0 „	Various			Cast off & proceeded 4·15 Cleared boom Bar 29·
4·55 „	N E x ❧			Cape Irene abm dis 2' Ofc N E x E.
7·50 „	N E x N			„ Kephalo abm dis 2' Ofc N E x N
9·15 „				Entered outer nets delay caused by mark
				boat not showing light 10·0 Entered boom
10·20				Made fast alongside "Hulk" & commenced
				disch troops etc. 11·0 All troops finished
	Distance Run			Commander Mate E. W. Wooln
				disembarking commenced disch cargo.

Hours.	Courses.	Speed.	Winds.	*Saturday* REMARKS. 4th *December 1915*
6·30 AM			Various	Commenced embarking sick 7·0 Finished
			„	disch all cargo took in mails.
7·50 „	S W x S		Sky	Left Hulk & proceeded out. 8·20 Cleared net corry
	„ „		„	Light breeze fine clear 29·78
8·55 „	S W x W		„	Cape Irene abm dis 2' Ofc S W X W.
9·0 „			„	Ofc S W x W ½ W 11·40 Cape Irene abm.
0·40 PM			„	Entered boom. 1·0 Anchored off R E p
1·30 „			„	Motor lighter for sick. 4·35 All sick
			„	disembarked weighed anchor
4·55 „			„	Made fast alongside Queen Alexandra
6·0 „			„	Comm bunkering. Crew employed coaling
8·0 „			„	Finished „ for the night
			„	Light breeze fine cloudy. Bar 29·87
	Distance Run			Commander Mate E. W. Wooln

The calm after the storm. The log of HMS *BARRY* for 3rd and 4th December 1915; a few days after she had battled through the worst weather conditions experienced in the northern Aegean for many years.

PRO Ref: ADM53/34830

19th December and the *BARRY* played a prominent part in the evacuation of Suvla. In company with the transport, *PRINCESS ENA*, she stood alongside the embarkation stage and took on troops as fast as they arrived. The first contingent was transferred to the battleship, *MAGNIFICENT*, while others were taken to Imbros or to Mudros Bay. She worked quickly and efficiently, the superintending beach master complimenting Commander Venning on his smart work. The evacuation was frequently interrupted by shell and rifle fire from the enemy, despite the fact that they were unaware of what exactly was happening, but the *BARRY* safely took off the rearguard and was one of the last ships to leave Suvla Bay. She sailed at 01.10 on Monday 20th December and anchored in Kephalo harbour at 02.40. The beach master and his assistants set fire to the remaining stores and set off in a naval pinnace; the operation had been successfully completed by 04.00 that morning.

After discharging the last of the troops the *BARRY* remained in Kephalo harbour, where, over the next couple of weeks, she underwent an overhaul by her crew. On Wednesday 22nd December she resumed her supply duties, sailing between Mudros and Imbros, until the start of the evacuation of Helles Beach on Tuesday 28th December. The *BARRY* arrived off Helles at 19.15 on Saturday 1st January 1916, and began taking troops on board from lighters which brought them from the shore. Their embarkation was made difficult by the rough sea and the lighters damaged several of her hull plates while lying alongside, causing a number of leaks. By midnight she had taken on her full complement but it was not until 03.30 on the Sunday that she was able to depart, owing to difficulties in raising and boarding her anchor. At 10.00 she anchored in Mudros Bay but was prohibited from taking any further part in the operation owing to her leaking hull. The evacuation of Helles Beach was completed by the early hours of 9th January 1916, like that of Suvla and Anzac, without loss of life; the successful conclusion of an abortive adventure.

After the Dardanelles

Although the Gallipoli campaign had ended, a presence in the Eastern Mediterranean was still necessary and semi-permanent garrisons remained on Lemnos, Imbros and Tenedos. The *BARRY*, after temporary repairs to her plates, returned to her former duties, carrying supplies and personnel between Mudros Bay and Kephalo harbour.

She had been running hard since her arrival in the Aegean with scarcely any time for maintenance, but on Saturday 18th March 1916 she left her station for a thorough overhaul at the shipyards at Ermoupolis, on the island of Syros. The log book states:-

"Saturday 18th March 1916.
17.30   Left Mudros Bay. Set log.
19.55   Cape Tripiti, (Strati Island), abeam.
23.22   Point Lithari, (Skyros), abeam. Log 60 miles.

Sunday 19th March 1916.
03.35   Cape Phassa, (Andros), abeam.
06.55   Arrived at Syros. Log 131 miles.
          Repairs and refurbishments carried out by crew
          and dockyard workers.

Following completion of her overhaul she left Ermoupolis on the morning of Sunday 21st May for a trial trip, anchoring in the harbour at Tinos for several hours. She returned to Syros that evening and on the following night sailed back to Mudros Bay. The log book records that her steaming time for the journey, of 9 hours 30 minutes, gave an average speed of 15.5 knots.

She then resumed running between Lemnos and Imbros, making one round trip daily. On Monday 30th October she was detailed to escort the submarine, E2; an hour after leaving Kephalo harbour a floating mine was sighted on the starboard bow. The two vessels stopped while the mine was sunk by rifle fire from the crew of E2. The submarine then led the *BARRY* for the rest of the journey to Mudros Bay.

Towards the end of 1916 she became employed on a wider sphere of operations, beginning on Tuesday 28th November, when she transported troops to and from the base on the island of Tenedos, followed in December by a visit to Salonika.

Ironically, the ending of the Gallipoli campaign did not free large numbers of troops for the Western Front as intended. Many were despatched to guard the Suez Canal against an expected Turkish attack and many more were stationed in northern Greece. During September 1915, while the Gallipoli campaign stagnated, the situation in the Balkan states became critical. Bulgaria joined the conflict on the side of Germany and Austria, an alliance which embodied plans for a campaign against Serbia. This act resulted in a commitment for the British and French, whereby they agreed to supply troops to assist Serbia. Although the Serbs had been overrun by early 1916, France maintained a presence at Salonika and the British government reluctantly agreed that an allied army should also remain in the area for the time being - a period which became extended to the whole duration of the war and which effectively interred 600,000 troops in northern Greece.

The *BARRY* was now required to assist in transporting personnel and supplies to and from the bases around the Gulf of Salonika. Her first visit took place on Friday 1st December 1916:-

"17.40   Left Mudros with mail.
18.22   Off Kastro Island.
23.25   Psathura Island light abeam

Saturday 2nd December.
04.45   Kassandra Point abeam.
09.10   Cape Kara light abeam.
09.20   Entered boom defence at Salonika harbour.
10.10   Arrived alongside HMS St. George,
                transferred mail.
16.45   Proceeded out of boom defence.
17.53   Epanomi light abeam.
21.10   Passed Kassandra light.

Sunday 3rd December.
01.45   Psathura light abeam.
07.10   Anchored off Australia Pier, Mudros Bay."

Her visits to Salonika became more and more frequent and she was based at the Greek city for a number of short spells; her main duties taking her to Kassandra, on the Halkidiki Peninsula, and also Katerini, a small town on the east coast of Greece, under Mount Olympus. In mid-December she returned to her Lemnos - Imbros sailings and on Christmas Eve 1916, once again, a floating mine appeared close alongside her starboard bow; it was destroyed by the crew using the three-pounder and rifle fire.

Throughout 1917 and 1918 her duties followed much the same pattern as those of late 1916 and proceeded with little incident. As time passed her role became less and less demanding and she spent many days at anchor in Mudros Bay, interspersed with occasional trips taking troops to Tarrant Bay, Lemnos, for gunnery practice.

In June 1917 personnel of the Mercantile Marine Reserve replaced her original crew. The men, who for over two years had faced the dangers from land, sea and air, were shipped aboard the battleship, *IMPLACABLE*, for Devonport.

At about the same time, America having joined the war in the previous April, the Bainbridge class destroyer, USS *BARRY*, joined the allied fleet in the Eastern Mediterranean. To avoid confusion the name of Campbell's *BARRY* was changed to *BARRYFIELD* and remained so for the duration of her naval service.

The Armistice with Turkey was signed aboard the battleship, *AGAMEMNON*, in Mudros Bay on 30th October 1918, but the *BARRYFIELD* was destined to remain in the Aegean for nearly another year, and her adventures were not yet over.

At 18.00 on Friday 14th February 1919 she left Salonika for Mudros Bay. At 23.50 she passed Kassandra; it was raining heavily and a fresh wind was blowing from the north-east. Vivid lightning flashed on the horizon and the weather looked very threatening. At 03.00 on Saturday 15th the wind dropped and a heavy swell rolled in from the south-east, the portent of an approaching storm; at 04.00 it struck! A sudden shift of wind brought a fierce gale and overwhelming seas from the south east. For seven hours she battled against the most appaling conditions, shipping tremendous seas which flooded the upper and main decks; the forepeak was making water rapidly owing to several of her plates near the stem having sprung open in a number of massive combers. A seaplane carrier approached and signalled that she would stand by her but there was little that she could do to help in the prevailing circumstances so she proceeded on her way. The log book continues:-

> "Saturday 15 February 1919.
> 08.15   Vessel labouring heavily in a most dangerous seaway. Seats, anchors and boats double-lashed down. Chief Engineer reported very short of coal - insufficient to reach Mudros. Commander ordered all available spare wood to be taken to stokehold. Wooden fenders and awning spars cut up and burned. Radio message for tug to assist."

The radio message was unanswered, but by 11.00 as she approached Lemnos, the lee of the island provided some shelter. Her commander, Lieut. M. Yates RNR, decided that in view of the sea conditions and the shortage of fuel he would not risk rounding Kombi Island and once again exposing the ship to the full fury of the storm. Instead he made for the harbour at Kondia, a village some miles east of Mudros Bay. Even in

154

this sheltered spot both anchors dragged and she had to be taken alongside the small pier where, at 16.15, she was secured for the night. Later that evening the minesweeping trawler, *JOHN BOWLER*, also came in for shelter and was able to provide the *BARRYFIELD* with two tons of water for her boiler, and three tons of coal which enabled her to proceed to Mudros when the weather moderated on Monday 17th. Once she was safely at anchor in the bay the crew pumped out her forepeak, which contained an alarming 5ft. 6ins. of water!

On Monday 24th March she was on her travels again, this time with supplies for Turkey. She left Mudros at 03.50 and exactly twelve hours later arrived in the harbour of Smyrna, (now Izmir), where she remained until the following Friday. A further overhaul took place at Ermoupolis, (Syros), between mid-April and the end of May; her release from Admiralty service was approaching. An examination of the log book for this period indicates that no effort was spared in ensuring that she was to be returned to her owners in the best possible condition; one entry reads, "Crew scraping paint off bridge brass and burning paint off teak deckhouse".

She left Mudros Bay for the last time at 18.25 on Friday 8th August 1919, and her departure from Greek waters followed a different route from that of her arrival four years before:-

"Saturday 9th August 1919.
09.45   Anchored off Piraeus.
16.00   Hove up.
18.30   Stopped for pilot.
18.40   Entered Corinth Canal.
19.12   Passed out of canal.

Sunday 10th August 1919.
05.00   Xante, (Zakinthos), abeam.

Monday 11th August 1919.
07.30   Entered Valletta harbour, Malta."

She remained at Valletta until sailing for the UK on Wednesday 27th August. After calling for coal and water at Algiers, Gibraltar and Corcubion, she passed Ushant at 04.50 on Sunday 7th September and arrived in Plymouth Sound at 15.15 on the same day.

In performing the duties which had taken her away to distant shores, she had been subjected to enemy attack, constant danger from mines and torpedoes, and extremes of weather - conditions for which she had never been intended. Nevertheless, she had survived and returned undaunted to rejoin her consorts in the Bristol Channel; but first came her lengthy refit. At 14.30 on Thursday 25th September 1919 she left Devonport and arrived at the Ailsa Shipbuilding Co's yard at Troon at mid-day on Saturday 27th, where, to quote the Bristol Channel & District Guide once more, "...the skilled hands of the shipbuilders and the delicate touches of the decorators eliminated the many, but honourable, wounds of war."

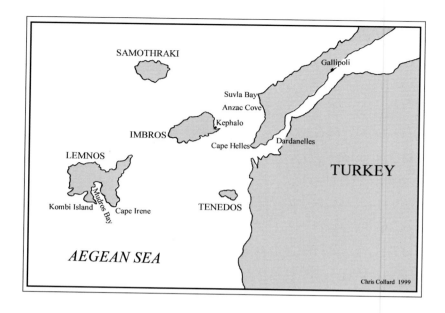

The principal areas served by HMS *BARRY/BARRYFIELD*, from 1915 to 1919.

KEEPING THE HOME FIRES BURNING

"The lamps are going out all over Europe. We shall not see them lit again in our lifetime."
Sir Edward Grey. British Foreign Secretary. 1914.

The "Golden Age" of the British paddle steamer ended in the summer of 1914. In the few years prior to the outbreak of the First World War, there were more such vessels running excursions around the coast of Great Britain than at any other time in history. The White Funnel Fleet enjoyed a popularity hitherto unknown and although the services were to continue after the conflict, the Great War ended an era never to be seen again.

On Wednesday 5th August 1914, the day after war was declared, the *ALBION* sailed from Brighton, Eastbourne and Hastings to Folkestone, but the harbour was so jammed with vessels that she was refused entry. Her passengers had to be content with a distant view of the animated scene on the quayside, with the movements of crowding refugees and the presence of military guards. The passage from Folkestone to Boulogne was the only route then open between England and France. The result was that the harbour was so choked with shipping that there was no berth left to be allotted to a pleasure steamer. On the same day the *BRIGHTON QUEEN* had sailed to Cowes and Southsea to witness the race between the big yachts for the "Emperor's Cup"; Cowes Week was in full swing!

The *BRIGHTON QUEEN* was scheduled to visit Boulogne on Thursday 6th August and a good crowd of passengers waited at Brighton for her 10.00 sailing, including many French people wishing to return home. Just half an hour before her departure time a telegram arrived from the Boulogne Harbourmaster stating that "it was highly preferable that the *BRIGHTON QUEEN* should not come", the harbour being too crowded. Her sailings for that day were therefore cancelled. On the following morning she made her way to Southampton, where she took on coal, before sailing light on the 8th August, arriving at Bristol on the following day. All further Boulogne trips were cancelled. Despite this disruption to the cross-channel sailings the coastal trips continued unhindered; the German mine-laying campaign had not yet reached the south coast.

On Monday 24th August the *RAVENSWOOD* developed a crack in the cover of her high pressure cylinder and limped into Eastbourne pier. The *ALBION* took her in tow to off Shoreham, from where the tug, *STELLA*, took her into the harbour; the White Funnel Fleet's usual south coast base, Newhaven, being too full. The *GLEN ROSA*, under the command of Capt. Hector McFadyen, was sent south to take over her sailings, leaving Bristol on Wednesday 26th August. After temporary repairs the *RAVENSWOOD* left Shoreham, under her own steam, on the morning of Saturday 29th August and arrived at Bristol on the following day. At the end of their season the *ALBION* docked in Bristol on Sunday 27th September and the *GLEN ROSA* arrived on the 28th; like the *BRIGHTON QUEEN*, neither vessel would sail on the south coast again.

Capt. Alec Campbell had reported to the directors, on Friday 7th August, that owing to the great falling off in the traffic during the Bank Holiday week, he had considered it advisable to lay up seven of the Bristol Channel steamers. The Cardiff to Weston ferry continued, while the regular service to Ilfracombe was maintained by the *LADY ISMAY* from Cardiff, and the *GLEN USK* from Bristol. The last trip of the season to Ilfracombe was made on Saturday 26th September and the ferry ended on the following Wednesday. An amusing incident from this period was related by Mr. Fred Birmingham, Campbells' Ilfracombe agent. One of the steamers was on a cruise along the North Devon coast when her purser arrested two suspected spies who were taking an unusual interest in the Bull Point lighthouse. When the steamer arrived at Ilfracombe, Mr. Birmingham was called on board to interview the "suspects" and found himself face to face with two of his close friends! They were immediately released.

Early in 1915 the "Ilfracombe Chronicle" printed the following paragraph:-

> "The Admiralty authorities at Devonport have declined to accede to the application of Messrs. P. & A. Campbell Ltd., to run a service of passenger steamers in the Bristol Channel this summer. It was intended to start the service with five steamers at Whitsuntide, but the Admiralty have refused permission, even though it was pointed out that the vessels would not ply below the Holms."

The Admiralty, however, later reconsidered its decision and permission was granted for steamer services to be made in the upper reaches of the channel, provided that the trips were run in daylight only. Accordingly, the *WAVERLEY* opened the Cardiff to Weston ferry, under the command of Capt. Joe Ashford, on Wednesday 19th May 1915.

On the following day the *RAVENSWOOD*, (Capt. Henry Chidgey), made a satisfactory trial trip from Bristol to Walton Bay, following the fitting of a new high pressure cylinder, and on Saturday 22nd May both she and the *ALBION*, (Capt. Dan Taylor), began sailing on the ferry.

These two steamers probably have the distinction of running the shortest seasons on record; on Whit-Sunday 23rd May they were requisitioned by the Admiralty. The *RAVENSWOOD* returned to Bristol on the night of Whit Monday followed by the *ALBION* on Wednesday 26th May. In the meantime the *GLEN ROSA*, (Capt. James Denman), was in service from Whit-Monday to Thursday 27th May. Capt. Dan Taylor took over the *WAVERLEY* from Joe Ashford on Thursday 10th June and she alone was sufficient to meet the demands of the travelling public until the *GLEN ROSA* re-entered service on Saturday 31st July, in time for the Bank Holiday.

At the board meeting on Thursday 8th July 1915 Capt. Peter reported on his recent visit to London for the purpose of inspecting the six Thames paddle steamers of the "Belle" fleet which were laid up in the East India Dock, in the hands of the liquidators of their owners, the Coast Development Corporation. The mortagees, Messrs. Denny, had written to P. & A. Campbell Ltd. and suggested that the company might like to consider their purchase. It was decided, however, that it was not advisable, at that stage, to entertain business of such magnitude. (Five of the Belle steamers were requisitioned by the Admiralty for minesweeping between 6th August 1915 and 7th April 1916).

The last trip "down channel" until 1919. Passengers aboard the *LADY ISMAY* at Ilfracombe on Saturday 26th September 1914.

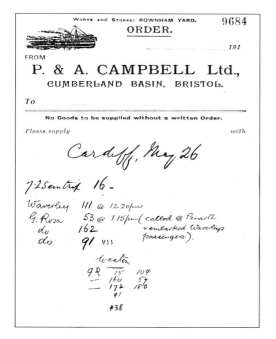

An example of the daily return sent from the Traffic Manager at Cardiff to Campbells' head office at Bristol. The passenger figures, as well as details of the "technical problems" aboard the *WAVERLEY*, would then have been entered into the memorandum book.

DIRECT DAILY EXPRESS SERVICE BETWEEN

WESTON AND CARDIFF

Calling at Penarth (passage 45 minutes)

By the Magnificent Saloon Steamers

"WAVERLEY" &
"GLEN ROSA,"

(Weather and circumstances permitting).

JULY, 1915.

LEAVE WESTON.	RETURN CARDIFF.
JULY	JULY
THU 15 10.30 am, ᴀ4.15, 6.30, *8.45 pm	THU 15 9.35 am, 12.0 noon, 5.30, 7.45 pm
FRI 16 10.30 am, ᴀ5.0, 8.15 pm	FRI 16 9.35 am, 12.30, 6.15 pm
SAT 17 ᴀ10.5 am, ᴀ12.5, ᴀ5.20, 7.35, *9.35 pm	SAT 17 9.15, 11.15 am, 1.15, 6.35, *8.45 pm
MON 19 *9.30 am, 12 noon, ᴀ6.0, *8.30 pm	MON 19 *8.40, 11.0 am, 2.30, 7.15 pm
TUE 20 10.30 am, 1.0, ᴀ6.30, *9.0 pm	TUE 20 9.35 am, 12.0 noon, 2.30, 7.45 pm
WED 21 10.30 am, 12.45, ᴀ3.5, *8.0 pm	WED 21 9.35, 11.45 am, 2.15, 4.20 pm
THU 22 10.45 am, 1.30, 4.15, *9.15 pm	THU 22 9.45 am, 12.30, 2.45, 5.30 pm
FRI 23 12.15, 3.0, 5.45 pm	FRI 23 11.15 am, 2.0, 4.30 pm
SAT 24 ᴀ11.30 am, ᴀ1.40, 4.15, 7.0 pm	SAT 24 *7.40 am, 12.40, 2.45, 5.30 pm
MON 26 *8.35 am, ᴀ2.15, 5.15, *8.0 pm	MON 26 *7.45, 9.45 am, 3.30, 6.30 pm
TUE 27 *9.20 am, ᴀ3.15, 5.30, *8.0 pm	TUE 27 *8.30, 10.30 am, 4.30, 6.45 pm
WED 28 *10.5 am, ᴀ4.0, 6.15, *8.30 pm	WED 28 *9.15, 11.15 am, 5.15, 7.30 pm
THU 29 10.30 am, ᴀ4.35, 7.0, *9.0 pm	THU 29 9.35 am, 12.0 noon, 5.50, *8.10 pm
FRI 30 10.30 am, ᴀ5.0, *7,45 pm	FRI 30 9.35 am, 12.30, 6.20 pm
SAT 31 9.30, *10.30, 11.45 am, *12.20, 5.45, *8.0, *8.15 pm	SAT 31 8.30, *9.35, 10.45, *11.30 am, 1.0, 1.15, 6.45, 7.0 pm

* Does not call at Penarth.   ᴀ These Steamers sail direct to Cardiff and call at Penarth on the next outward journey.

FARES—CARDIFF or PENARTH: Single 1/6, Return (day of issue) 2/-
Except on Saturday, July 31st, when the Fares will be Single 2/-, Return (day of issue) 2/6.

IMPORTANT NOTICE.
THE COMPANY CANNOT CONVEY ALIENS UNDER ANY CIRCUMSTANCES.

NOTE—Handbills of all Sailings may be obtained at BRUTON & Co's Music Warehouse, 70 High Street; C. E. MASTERS & Co, Estate Agents, South Parade; LEWIS WING, Ltd, Chemists, Magdala Buildings, Regent Street, Walliscote Road, and The Boulevard; The INFORMATION BUREAU, Sea Lawns; United Bill-posting Co., Ltd., 22 Waterloo Street.

Dogs, 1/- each way   Bicycles, Prams or Mail carts (at Owner's risk) 1/- Single or Return   Motor Bicycles (at Owner's risk) 2/- each way
Motor Bicycles and Side Cars, 4/- each way   Children under 12 years of age, Half-price   The Company reserve the right to alter the advertised time or withdraw any of the above sailings as weather or other circumstances may require   A reasonable quantity of Passengers' Luggage carried free of charge (at Owner's risk)   Passengers are requested to label same   "Bristol Channel District Guide," Official Handbook of P. & A. Campbell, Ltd, 300 illustrations, a mass of interesting matter—Price 4d, per post 7d.

Telegrams { "Ward, Pier Weston-super-Mare " / " Ravenswood, Bristol " / " Ravenswood, Cardiff "

Nat. Telephones—44 Weston, 3112 Bristol, 789 Cardiff, 550 Newport, 17 Clevedon, 87 Ilfracombe, 29 Lynmouth, 4 Minehead.

For further particulars apply to—R. H. WARD, Agent, Office, Pier Gates, Weston
W. GUY, Agent, 1 Stuart Street, Cardiff;
THOS. COOK & SON, 2 Duke Street, Cardiff; or
P. & A. CAMPBELL, Ltd., Cumberland Basin, Bristol.

* 5—200—3000   FRAMPTON & SONS, "Mercury" Offices, Waterloo Street, Weston-super-Mare.

A Cardiff timetable for 1915.

The seasons of 1915 and 1916 passed without incident with the *WAVERLEY* and *GLEN ROSA* in service between Cardiff and Weston, but with the requisitioning of those two steamers in May 1917 the entire White Funnel Fleet was now in the hands of the Admiralty. In order to maintain the ferry, the company chartered the small paddle steamer *DUCHESS OF DEVONSHIRE* from the Devon Dock, Pier & Steamship Co., of Exmouth. Terms for the charter, at £216 13s 4d per month, had been agreed by mid-May and she sailed from Exmouth to Cardiff to begin service at Whitsun 1917, manned by the P. & A. Campbell personnel who had been found unfit for Royal Naval service. Capt. Dan Taylor was master with Capt. Joe Ashford as Chief Officer; Capt. Henry Chidgey acted as Bosun, with Capt. James Bilson and, possibly, Capt. James Denman as deck hands. She was certificated to carry 450 passengers, and although she was rather slow and sometimes "hard pressed" to cope with the strong tides and currents of the Bristol Channel, her two wartime seasons were, nevertheless, accomplished satisfactorily.

Financial Matters.

During the Great War the excursion paddle steamers were hired from their companies by the Admiralty. The question of the cost of their hire is intriguing and one which cannot be answered in great detail. The existing records of P. & A. Campbell Ltd. are tantalisingly incomplete on the subject. The first reference to the financial situation appears in the minutes of the meeting of Monday 5th October 1914 and states:

> "The question of a rate of hire to be paid by the Admiralty for the Brighton Queen and Devonia was discussed. Alec suggested £1000 per month for each. The Admiralty mentioned £500 as a fair rate. It was left to Alec to arrange the best possible terms."

A figure of £600 per month was eventually agreed. No further reference appears until Monday 6th September 1915, when the minute book records:-

> "A letter was read from the Director of Transport suggesting a reduction in the rate of hire of the steamers requisitioned by the Admiralty. An appropriate letter was sent in reply."

Frustratingly, no elaboration as to the reply is recorded, but in the light of the next financial reference, the contents of the letter are not difficult to imagine:-

> "Thursday 10th February 1916. The rates of hire suggested by the Admiralty were discussed, but as they averaged only £316 per boat, per month, the board decided not to accept them; the secretary pointing out that the £600 originally fixed in the case of the Devonia was still being paid monthly."

Further records show, however, that the rate for the *DEVONIA* was £350 monthly from 1st January 1917.

On Monday 2nd July 1917 the directors declined the offer of £22,800 per year for the hire of the whole fleet but decided to "stand out for £400 per boat, per month". Two months later a further offer was made by the Admiralty of £30,000 per year for the hire of the whole fleet. Capt. Alec was not present at the meeting but was immediately sent the following wire:-

> "Directors very strongly of opinion should accept Admiralty offer at once, as Raeburn of the Admiralty, advises. John Cory, Director, fears possible withdrawal of offer as happened in case of one of his ships".

Whether or not the offer was accepted is not stated and no further details of the hiring costs appear.

The question of compensation for the loss of the *BRIGHTON QUEEN* and *LADY ISMAY* was also the subject of protracted negotiations, which first began in November 1915. The terms offered by the Ministry of Shipping were eventually accepted on Monday 5th November 1917 and amounted to £29,500 for the three-year old *LADY ISMAY*, and £22,500 for the eighteen-year old *BRIGHTON QUEEN*.

As a final footnote on financial matters, two minute book entries which reflect the ethos of the time are quoted:-

> "Monday 6th September 1915. Mr. Handcock suggested that wounded soldiers should be allowed a free trip by steamer on certain days, also a cup of tea with bread and butter. This was agreed".

> "Monday 7th August 1916. It was noted that the company had paid £30 for the entertainment of 200 soldiers at Bristol Zoo".

New Ships for Old.

In 1918 the company approached the Ministry of Shipping with regard to the purchase of an additional vessel and in September the Ministry offered the *WOOLWICH BELLE*, the smallest of the London based Belle Steamers, and the only member of the fleet not requisitioned by the Admiralty. The minutes of the directors meeting of Monday 16th September 1918 state:-

> "Capt. Peter gave an account of the present condition of the Woolwich Belle, expressing the opinion that about £6500 to £7000 would probably purchase her as she lies. He also explained that there would be a great expense in obtaining a Board of Trade certificate for the Duchess of Devonshire next season. It was eventually agreed that negotiations with a view to purchasing the Woolwich Belle should proceed."

It is unclear why there would have been "great expense" in obtaining a Board of Trade certificate for the *DUCHESS OF DEVONSHIRE*, but she was, nevertheless, chartered for the 1919 season and supplemented the sailings of the steamers as they returned to civilian service. Her charter ended in October 1919, when she was returned to her owners at Exmouth.

The *DUCHESS OF DEVONSHIRE*, arriving at Weston-Super-Mare. 1917/1919.

Photographs of the *DUCHESS OF DEVONSHIRE* in the Bristol Channel are extremely rare. Those reproduced on this page are included for their "novelty" value rather than any significant addition to the pictorial history of the ship. Above:- The Mountstuart Dry Dock Co's pontoon is being towed into position at Cardiff; in the top, left-hand corner of the photograph, the *DUCHESS* can be seen lying at the Pier Head. Below:- In this view of two tugs undergoing maintenance in Stothert's dry dock at Bristol, the foremast, bridge and funnel of the *DUCHESS* are visible in the background.

No further developments took place with regard to the purchase of the *WOOLWICH BELLE*; no doubt the impending cessation of hostilities and return of the company's fleet made a further purchase inadvisable at that stage. Nevertheless, as the company set about planning for its future it became obvious that additional tonnage was necessary. Apart from the loss of the *BRIGHTON QUEEN* and *LADY ISMAY*, the surveys of the *WAVERLEY, GLEN ROSA* and *ALBION* revealed that their war service had taken its toll; they were beyond economical repair and destined for the breaker's yard. The *GLEN ROSA* and *WAVERLEY* were laid up in Bristol until Friday 1st October 1920 when, under the supervision of Capt. Allan Livingstone, they were towed up the Floating Harbour, the *GLEN ROSA* to Gas House Point, and the *WAVERLEY* to Great Western Point, where they were broken up by Pugsley & Co.

In October 1919 an order was placed with the Ailsa Shipbuilding Co., of Troon for a new vessel - an enlarged version of the *GLEN USK*. The launching of the ship, *GLEN GOWER*, lay some years ahead but she was to receive several legacies from three of her predecessors.

The *ALBION* was broken up at Troon during the course of 1920, but her 26 year old engine was dismantled and taken into the Ailsa Co's workshop for inspection. The bearings were micrometer measured and those which were worn were replaced: a new, low pressure cylinder slide valve was fitted and the whole engine was re-assembled and checked for alignment. Despite the fact that the fire caused by the bombing attack at Dunkirk in 1917 had twisted the framework of the after part of the ship, the engine had escaped damage and was held in storage for subsequent installation into the new steamer. The whole operation - Ailsa Contract No. 112 - cost in excess of £18,000: a considerable sum, but cheaper than a new engine!

Other items inherited by the *GLEN GOWER* were the *ALBION'S* binnacle, compass, engine room telegraphs, steering engine, several lower deck ports, and her bell - the name *ALBION* being ground out and *GLEN GOWER* engraved in its place. Even the lost steamers were not to be forgotten. She inherited the small ladder which led from the promenade deck to the quarter deck at the stern of the *LADY ISMAY*, which had been removed and held in storage at Bristol since the ship had been converted for minesweeping in 1914. But perhaps the most unusual item of her legacy was the cash register which, in the halcyon pre-war days, rang out in the bar of the sadly missed *BRIGHTON QUEEN*

The *ALBION* being broken up at Troon in 1920.

POSTSCRIPT

The Pockett Steamers.

In the last few seasons before the Great War began, the only excursion steamers operating in the Bristol Channel, other than those of the White Funnel Fleet, were the two vessels owned by Pockett's Bristol Channel Steam Packet Co. Ltd., of Bristol. They were the *MAVIS* and the *BRIGHTON*, both of which maintained a service between their base at Swansea and, principally, the resorts of North Devon.

Owing to engine trouble the MAVIS did not run in 1914 and spent the year laid up at Bristol. She was not requisitioned by the Admiralty and was sold for breaking up in 1915. Her final journey took her to Briton Ferry, in tow of the tug, *KLONDYKE*, on March 22nd of that year.

The *BRIGHTON* was not called up immediately but completed her 1914 season and was requisitioned in March 1915 to take part in the Dardanelles campaign. Her forward well deck was boarded over with wood planking and she left Bristol on 29th July, calling at Ilfracombe on the following day. By 10th August she had reached Oporto and, after a call at Gibraltar, made her way to Malta where, in Valletta Harbour, she was converted into a water carrier. When she arrived at the island of Lemnos is not certain but records show that on 27th September 1915 she was coaling with the *BARRY* from a collier in Mudros Bay.

She continued her water supplying duties until after the evacuation of Gallipoli, when she returned to Malta for fitting out as a minelayer. From then on her movements are uncertain until 11th June 1917 when she was purchased from Pockett's by the Controller of Shipping on behalf of the Admiralty. By the beginning of 1919 she appears to have been surplus to requirements and remained laid up in Mudros Bay; the final entry in her final log book, (the only one which has survived), states:-

> "Monday 10th February 1919.
> At Mudros. All personnel left. Nobody left on board HMS Brighton."

At the end of the year the Admiralty sold her to Turkish owners and she continued to run in the Aegean and the Sea of Marmora until being broken up in 1927.

The Fate of the "Racecourse" Class.

Of the thirty-two "progeny" of the *GLEN USK*, five had been lost during the war and one was sold in 1919 to the James Dredging Co. Ltd., of London, but was broken up soon after the sale. The remaining vessels were laid up. One of them, HMS *ATHERSTONE*, was purchased by the New Medway Steam Packet Co. of Rochester in 1927 and re-named *QUEEN OF KENT*. The rest were sold to various shipbreakers at about the same time, from one of whom the New Medway Co. bought a second, HMS *MELTON*, re-naming her *QUEEN OF THANET*. As E. C. B. Thornton states in "South Coast Pleasure Steamers" :-

> "It seems such a very great pity that twenty-four perfectly good paddle
> steamers were allowed to rot at their moorings by the Admiralty for some

eight years, and then scrapped, when they could have been sold or even given to the companies in replacement of their steamers sunk in the First World War."

The *QUEEN OF KENT* and *QUEEN OF THANET* were suitably converted for their peacetime roles and were given raked masts and funnels. They proved to be excellent pleasure steamers and became very popular on their regular excursions between Rochester, Margate, Ramsgate, and occasional cross-channel trips. More radical changes took place in 1931 when they were given larger paddle wheels and were converted to oil firing.

They served in the Second World War, initially as minesweepers but later in a variety of capacities, and reverted to their former duties on the Thames and Medway in 1946. Three years later a further change of ownership took them to the south coast when they joined the Red Funnel Company, of Southampton. The *QUEEN OF KENT* became the *LORNA DOONE* and was based at Bournemouth, while the *QUEEN OF THANET* became the *SOLENT QUEEN* and was based at Southampton. Their 1949 and 1950 seasons were most succesful but disaster struck in 1951.

On 22nd June, just before entering service, the *SOLENT QUEEN* caught fire while undergoing overhaul on the slip at Southampton. The after part of the ship was burnt out and the damage was so extensive that she was considered to be beyond economic repair. She remained laid up for the summer and was broken up during October of that year.

The *LORNA DOONE* completed the 1951 season without incident but during the following winter she was deemed to have reached the end of her useful life and was broken up in March 1952. Ironically, when the *GLEN USK*, two years older than the first "Racecourse" paddle steamer, was withdrawn from service at the end of 1960, she had outlived the last of her "offspring" by nine years.

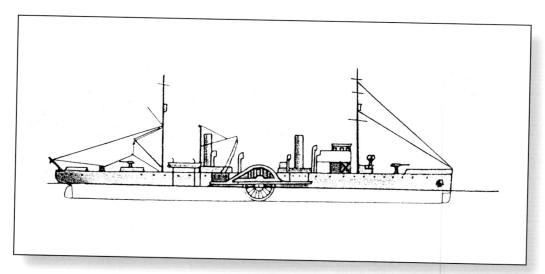

The Pockett steamer *BRIGHTON* at Ilfracombe on 30th July 1915 on her way from Bristol to the Eastern Mediterranean. The white hut on the pier was Campbells' ticket office - closed until further notice.

HMS *BRIGHTON* in Mudros Bay, Lemnos. A washing line has been slung between the foremast and the bridge - even amid the stern necessities of war domestic matters were not forgotten.

A WARSHIP CONVERSION

The New Medway Steam Packet Company having been quite successful in converting the paddle minesweeper *Atherstone* into the pleasure steamer *Queen of Kent*, they are venturing to repeat the experiment, and have purchased her sister ship the *Melton* for similar treatment during the coming winter. Hitherto none of the owners of excursion steamers have shown the least inclination to buy these paddlers for conversion, although it has often been suggested to them by the Admiralty contracts department, but this enterprising concern appears to have got an excellent bargain, and the *Queen of Kent* has already proved herself exceedingly popular on excursions to the Kent coast and across the Channel to France.

M.S.R. July 1928

The new Medway steamer "QUEEN OF KENT" (see above)

CONVERSION OF MINESWEEPERS

In the July number of the "Merchant Shipping Review" we produced a photograph showing the *Queen of Kent*, the paddle steamer which the New Medway Steam Packet Company has found most successful for coastal and cross-channel excursion trips this season.

She was originally one of the paddle minesweepers built in the middle of the war for the express purpose of passing right over an enemy minefield with a shallow draught. Quite a number of these ships have been retained on the reserve when their consorts of other classes went to the scrappers, and there has always been a certain measure of surprise that excursion steamship companies have not taken them up more enthusiastically.

Encouraged by the success of the *Queen of Kent*, which has proved herself a most successful vessel, the New Medway Company has purchased one of her sister ships, the *Melton*, which is being converted in similar fashion at Rochester. The photograph shows her alongside the quay, and is interesting for comparison with the photograph of the *Queen of Kent* published in July.

M.S.R. SEPT. 1928

Two articles which were published in the nautical press in July and September 1928 regarding the conversion of the Racecourse paddlers.

PHOTOGRAPH. BY.

The "Queen of Kent"

WILLIS, 67 HIGH ST CHATHAM

The *QUEEN OF KENT*, (ex. HMS *ATHERSTONE*), in the Thames estuary in the 1930's.

EPILOGUE

When in peacetime ye of England,
On pleasure bent once more,
Cross that stretch of channel water
Which spreads from shore to shore,
In thought, at least, salute anew
Those tombed below who died for you
And England in the war.

From one of the "Ballads of the Dover Patrol".

The return of peace. With Capt. Dan Taylor in command, the CAMBRIA, packed to capacity, passes Battery
Point, Portishead, on the first post-war trip from Bristol to Ilfracombe. Saturday 2nd August 1919.

SUBSCRIBERS.

The author wishes to express his sincere thanks to the persons listed below for their support of the "White Funnels" series.

Lt. Cdr. R. K. P. Abbott RNR
Mr. J. R. Adams
K. M. Adams
Mr. M. H. Adams
Crawford Alexander
Myra and John Allen
Tom Allison
K. Allwright
Dr. Don Anderson
Allan C. Baker
Tom Baker
Michael Courtenay Banks
Bernard Barry
David J. Barton
Michael Bawden
David Beeney
R. W. Beesley
Norman D. Bird
Sqn. Ldr. Alan Birt
Jeff Bishop
G. G. Boswell
A. J. Bracey
D. S. Braisted
J. C. Brewer
Alan J. Bridges
W. G. Brown
W. Haydn Burgess
David Burt
Kenneth John Campbell
Tony Carless
Eric H. Chamberlain
Richard Clammer
Peter Clark
Bob Coles
Mr. Alex Collard
Marion and Terence Collard
Rosemary Collard
Andrew Collier
Nigel Coombes
P. E. Cox
Mr. Terry Creswell
John E. Cronin
R. G. Cunningham
Alister Currie
Richard Danielson
Malcolm Darch
E. I. Dare
Capt. Ted Davies
Mr. E. G. Davis
S. P. Denby
David Docherty
J. Donaldson
Alan Downs
Keith Draper
Dr. R. A. S. Dunn
Mrs. R. A. Durston
Steve Dutfield
Roger F. V. Edlin
Brian Elliott
Christopher Evans
Ian Evans
L. J. Evans
R. A. Fenner
James A. Fisher
Kenneth F. Fisher

Adrian Flower
Kenneth Floyd
Kenneth Fraser
Eric Freeman
P. J. Fricker
Maurice Gambling
G. F. A. Gilbert
Andrew Gladwell
T. A. Glasson
Mr. G. A Gough
Mr. Crispin Graves
Syd Gray
Victor Gray
John L. Green
Andrew Gully
John Hall
Mr. F. Hann
Mr. & Mrs. A. R. Harvey
Mr. David Harvey
R. L. Havard
Chris Henton
J. P. Henworth
Dr. David T. Herriot
C. Hinton
John and Elizabeth Holmes
Leslie and Sylvia Homer
Keith Hooper
Mr. Tony Horn
Rev. Jack House
Kenneth Howell
Rev. A. W. Huckett
G. A. Jacobs
G. E. Jefferies
K. W. Jenkins
Mr. B. Jones
Don K. Jones
Mr. J. Jones
John Jones
Mr N. Jones
P. D. A. Joziasse
John Kelly BEM.
R. Kenney
G. Burnham Lee
Tom S. B. Lee
Alec Lewis
Howard Lewis
Geoffrey C. Lidstone
John G. Lidstone
Ian Maclagan
Alastair Reid McMillan
M. J. Mason
P. K. Massey
J. L. May
John May
John Mead
David J. Mills
Dr. Harold Mills
H. R. A. Mills
Anthony J. Morgan
D. R. Morris
Mrs. F. D. Morris
Andrew P. Munn
Martin Nelson
John Niblett
Roger Nowell

Martin Oatway
Mr. H. G. Owen
Raymond M. Palmer
Michael Parsons
Norman Partyn
Brian Patton
C. H. Pearce
R. Pinfield
Roger and Diane Pollard
M. H. Pook
Robert S. Purcell
Geoffrey Purrier
Ian Ramsay
L. Gordon Reed
Stan and Joan Rendell
T. G. Richards
Mike Riley
Sidney Robinson
A. J. Salter
John Salvage
Ken Saunders
Dr. Ernst Schmidt
Clive Seaton
G. J. Shaw
Colin M. Simpson
Ron Sims
J. K. W. Slater
Mrs Irma Smele
Mr. Clifford Smith
Mr. F. M. Smith
P. Southcombe
Hammy Sparks
Jean Spells
Derek Spiers
Clive Staddon
Paul Steeds
Michael Sullivan
Mike Tedstone
K. Thomas
Eric Tilly
Phillip H. Tolley
George C. Train
David Tribe
Charles Turner
Richard Turner
R. H. Turner
William S. Upcott
W. S. Vanstone
Alan Wakeman
Dr. W. M. Walker
Derek Warman
Mr. A. G. Webber
Henry West
A. S. Whiley
Miss Gwyneth White
Brian M. Whitmore
Mr. W. A. Widden
Ken and Rita Williams
M. J. Williams
Stephen Alan Williamson
Stephen J. Wilson
The Revd. Hal Wilton
Gordon Wood
Raymond Wood
Noel Woodman

The author also wishes to express his thanks to those persons whose subscriptions were received after this book closed for press.